Norman Bettger

Rosthern Sask.

Box 405.

Aug. 23 1949 - 50 - 51

Mrs Kostyna.

Janet Kostyna

SENIOR CATECHISM

LUTHER'S SMALL CATECHISM
IN
QUESTION AND ANSWER FORM

By J. A. Dell, D.D.

THE WARTBURG PRESS
Columbus 15, Ohio

Eleventh Printing

Copyright, 1939

THE LUTHERAN BOOK CONCERN

PRINTED
IN
U.S.A.

LUTHER'S SMALL CATECHISM

THE TWELVE YEAR OLD JESUS IN THE TEMPLE

LUTHER'S SMALL CATECHISM

PART I
THE TEN COMMANDMENTS

THE INTRODUCTION
I am the Lord thy God.

THE FIRST COMMANDMENT
Thou shalt have no other gods before Me.

What does this mean?
ANSWER: We should fear, love, and trust in God above all things.

THE SECOND COMMANDMENT
Thou shalt not take the name of the Lord thy God in vain, for the Lord will not hold him guiltless that taketh His name in vain.

What does this mean?
ANSWER: We should fear and love God so that we do not curse, swear, conjure, lie, or deceive, by His name, but call upon Him in every time of need, and worship Him with prayer, praise, and thanksgiving.

THE THIRD COMMANDMENT
Remember the Sabbath day, to keep it holy.

What does this mean?
ANSWER: We should fear and love God so that we do not despise His Word and the preaching of the same, but deem it holy, and gladly hear and learn it.

(5)

THE FOURTH COMMANDMENT

Honor thy father and thy mother, that thy days may be long upon the land which the Lord thy God giveth thee.

What does this mean?

ANSWER: We should fear and love God so that we do not despise our parents and superiors, nor provoke them to anger, but honor, serve, obey, love and esteem them.

THE FIFTH COMMANDMENT

Thou shalt not kill.

What does this mean?

ANSWER: We should fear and love God so that we do our neighbor no bodily harm nor cause him any suffering, but help and befriend him in every need.

THE SIXTH COMMANDMENT

Thou shalt not commit adultery.

What does this mean?

ANSWER: We should fear and love God so that we lead a chaste and pure life in word and deed, and that husband and wife love and honor each other.

THE SEVENTH COMMANDMENT

Thou shalt not steal.

What does this mean?

ANSWER: We should fear and love God so that we do not rob our neighbor of his money or property, nor bring them into our possession by unfair dealing or fraud, but help him to improve and protect his property and living.

THE EIGHTH COMMANDMENT

Thou shalt not bear false witness against thy neighbor.

What does this mean?

ANSWER: We should fear and love God so that we do not deceitfully belie, betray, backbite, nor slander our neighbor, but apologize for him, speak well of him, and put the most charitable construction on all that he does.

THE NINTH COMMANDMENT

Thou shalt not covet thy neighbor's house.

What does this mean?

ANSWER: We should fear and love God so that we do not seek by craftiness to gain possession of our neighbor's inheritance or home, nor obtain them under pretense of a legal right, but assist and serve him in keeping the same.

THE TENTH COMMANDMENT

Thou shalt not covet thy neighbor's wife, nor his manservant, nor his maidservant, nor his cattle, nor anything that is thy neighbor's.

What does this mean?

ANSWER: We should fear and love God so that we do not estrange or entice away our neighbor's wife, servants, or cattle, but seek to have them remain and discharge their duty to him.

THE CONCLUSION

What does God declare concerning all these Commandments?

ANSWER: He says: "I the Lord thy God am a jealous God, visiting the iniquity of the fathers upon the children unto the third and fourth generation of them that hate Me; and showing mercy unto thousands of them that love Me and keep My commandments."

What does this mean?

ANSWER: God threatens to punish all who transgress these commandments. We should, therefore, fear His wrath, and in no wise disobey them. But He promises grace and every blessing to all who keep them. We should, therefore, love Him, trust in Him, and gladly keep His commandments.

PART II

THE CREED

THE FIRST ARTICLE

OF CREATION

I believe in God the Father Almighty, maker of heaven and earth.

What does this mean?

ANSWER: I believe that God has created me and all that exists; that He has given and still preserves to me my body and soul, my eyes and ears, and all my members, my reason and all the powers of my soul, together with food and raiment, home and family, and all my property; that He daily provides abundantly for all the needs of my life, protects me from all danger, and guards and keeps me from all evil; and that He does this purely out of fatherly and divine goodness and mercy, without any merit or worthiness in me; for all which I am in duty bound to thank, praise, serve, and obey Him. This is most certainly true.

THE SECOND ARTICLE

OF REDEMPTION

And in Jesus Christ His only Son, our Lord; who was conceived by the Holy Ghost, born of the Virgin Mary; suffered under Pontius Pilate, was crucified, dead

and buried; He descended into hell; the third day He rose again from the dead; He ascended into heaven, and sitteth on the right hand of God the Father Almighty; from thence He shall come to judge the quick and the dead.

What does this mean?

ANSWER: I believe that Jesus Christ, true God, begotten of the Father from eternity, and also true Man, born of the Virgin Mary, is my Lord; who has redeemed me, a lost and condemned creature, bought me and freed me from all sins, from death, and from the power of the devil; not with silver and gold, but with His holy and precious blood, and with His innocent sufferings and death; in order that I might be His own, live under Him in His kingdom, and serve Him in everlasting righteousness, innocence, and blessedness; even as He is risen from the dead, and lives and reigns to all eternity. This is most certainly true.

THE THIRD ARTICLE

OF SANCTIFICATION

I believe in the Holy Ghost; the holy Christian Church, the communion of saints; the forgiveness of sins; the resurrection of the body; and the life everlasting. Amen.

What does this mean?

ANSWER: I believe that I cannot by my own reason or strength believe in Jesus Christ my Lord, or come to Him; but the Holy Ghost has called me through the Gospel, enlightened me with His gifts, and sanctified and preserved me in the true faith; in like manner as He calls, gathers, enlightens, and sanctifies the whole Christian Church on earth, and preserves it in union with Jesus Christ in the one true faith; in which Christian Church He daily forgives abundantly all my sins, and the sins of all believers, and at the last day will raise up me and all the dead, and will grant everlasting life to me and to all who believe in Christ. This is most certainly true.

PART III

THE LORD'S PRAYER

THE INTRODUCTION
Our Father, who art in heaven.

What does this mean?
ANSWER: God thereby tenderly encourages us to believe that He is truly our Father, and that we are truly His children, so that we may boldly and confidently come to Him in prayer, even as beloved children come to their dear father.

THE FIRST PETITION
Hallowed be Thy name.

What does this mean?
ANSWER: God's name is indeed holy in itself; but we pray in this petition that it may be hallowed also among us.

How is this done?
ANSWER: When the Word of God is taught in its truth and purity, and we, as God's children, lead holy lives, in accordance with it. This grant us, dear Father in heaven! But whoever teaches and lives otherwise than as God's Word teaches, profanes the name of God among us. From this preserve us, heavenly Father!

THE SECOND PETITION
Thy kingdom come.

What does this mean?

ANSWER: The kingdom of God comes indeed of itself, without our prayer; but we pray in this petition that it may also come to us.

How is this done?

ANSWER: When our heavenly Father gives us His Holy Spirit, so that by His grace we believe His holy Word, and live a godly life here on earth, and in heaven for ever.

THE THIRD PETITION
Thy will be done on earth, as it is in heaven.

What does this mean?

ANSWER: The good and gracious will of God is done indeed without our prayer; but we pray in this petition that it may also be done among us.

How is this done?

ANSWER: When God destroys and brings to naught every evil counsel and purpose of the devil, the world, and our own flesh, which would hinder us from hallowing His name, and prevent the coming of His kingdom; and when He strengthens us and keeps us steadfast in His Word and in faith, even unto our end. This is His good and gracious will.

THE FOURTH PETITION
Give us this day our daily bread.

What does this mean?

ANSWER: God indeed gives daily bread to all men, even to the wicked, without our prayer; but we pray in this petition that He would lead us to acknowledge our daily bread as His gift, and to receive it with thanksgiving.

What is meant by daily bread?

ANSWER: Everything that is required to satisfy our bodily needs; such as food and raiment, house and home, fields and flocks, money and goods; pious parents, children and servants; godly and faithful rulers, good government; seasonable weather, peace and health; order and honor; true friends, good neighbors, and the like.

THE FIFTH PETITION

And forgive us our trespasses, as we forgive those who trespass against us.

What does this mean?

ANSWER: We pray in this petition that our heavenly Father would not regard our sins nor because of them deny our prayers; for we neither merit, nor deserve those things for which we pray; but that He would grant us all things through grace, even though we sin daily, and deserve nothing but punishment. And certainly we, on our part, will heartily forgive, and gladly do good to those who may sin against us.

THE SIXTH PETITION

And lead us not into temptation.

What does this mean?

ANSWER: God indeed tempts no one to sin; but we pray in this petition that God would so guard and preserve us, that the devil, the world, and our own flesh, may not deceive us, nor lead us into error and unbelief, despair, and other great and shameful sins; but that, when so tempted, we may finally prevail and gain the victory.

THE SEVENTH PETITION

But deliver us from evil.

What does this mean?

ANSWER: We pray in this petition, as in a summary, that our heavenly Father would deliver us from all manner of evil, whether it affect the body or soul, property or reputation, and at last, when the hour of death shall come, grant us a blessed end, and graciously take us from this world of sorrow to Himself in heaven.

THE CONCLUSION

For Thine is the kingdom, and the power, and the glory, for ever and ever. Amen.

What does the word "Amen" mean?

ANSWER: It means that I should be assured that such petitions are acceptable to our heavenly Father, and are heard by Him; for He Himself has commanded us to pray in this manner, and has promised to hear us. Amen, Amen, that is, Yea, yea, it shall be so.

PART IV

THE SACRAMENT OF HOLY BAPTISM

I

What is Baptism?

ANSWER: Baptism is not simply water, but it is the water used according to God's command and connected with God's word.

What is this word of God?

ANSWER: It is the word of our Lord Jesus Christ, as recorded in the last chapter of Matthew:

"Go ye therefore, and make disciples of all the
nations, baptizing them into the name of the Father,
and of the Son, and of the Holy Spirit."

II

What gifts or benefits does Baptism bestow?

Answer: It works forgiveness of sins, delivers from
death and the devil, and gives everlasting salvation to all
who believe, as the word and promise of God declare.

What is this word and promise of God?

Answer: It is the word of our Lord Jesus Christ, as
recorded in the last chapter of Mark:

"He that believeth and is baptized shall be saved;
but he that believeth not shall be damned."

III

How can water do such great things?

Answer: It is not the water, indeed, that does such
great things, but the word of God connected with the
water, and our faith which relies on that word of God.
For without the word of God, it is simply water and no
baptism. But when connected with the word of God it is
a baptism, that is, a gracious water of life and a washing
of regeneration in the Holy Ghost, as St. Paul says to
Titus, in the third chapter:

"According to His mercy He saved us, by the washing of regeneration, and renewing of the Holy Ghost;
which He shed on us abundantly through Jesus Christ
our Savior; that being justified by His grace, we should
be made heirs according to the hope of eternal life.
This is a faithful saying."

IV

What does such baptizing with water signify?

ANSWER: It signifies that the old Adam in us, together with all sins and evil lusts, should be drowned by daily sorrow and repentance, and be put to death; and that the new man should daily come forth and rise, to live before God in righteousness and holiness for ever.

Where is it so written?

ANSWER: St. Paul, in the sixth chapter of the Epistle to the Romans, says:

"We are buried with Christ by baptism into death, that like as He was raised up from the dead by the glory of the Father, even so we also should walk in newness of life."

OF CONFESSION

What is Confession?

ANSWER: Confession consists of two parts: the one is, that we confess our sins; the other, that we receive absolution or forgiveness from the pastor as from God Himself, in no wise doubting, but firmly believing, that our sins are thereby forgiven before God in heaven.

What sins should we confess?

ANSWER: Before God we should acknowledge ourselves guilty of all manner of sins, even of those of which we are not aware, as we do in the Lord's Prayer. To the pastor we should confess only those sins which we know and feel in our hearts.

What are such sins?

ANSWER: Here examine yourself in the light of the Ten Commandments, whether as father or mother, son or daughter, master or servant, you have been disobedient, unfaithful, slothful, ill-tempered, unchaste, or quarrelsome, or whether you have injured any one by word or deed, stolen, neglected or wasted aught, or done any other evil.

THE OFFICE OF THE KEYS

What is the Office of the Keys?

ANSWER: It is the peculiar church power which Christ has given to His Church on earth to forgive the sins of penitent sinners, and to retain the sins of the impenitent so long as they do not repent.

What are the words of our Lord Jesus Christ
concerning the Office of the Keys?

ANSWER: Thus writes the holy evangelist John in the twentieth chapter: The Lord Jesus breathed on His disciples and saith unto them, Receive ye the Holy Ghost. Whose soever sins ye remit, they are remitted unto them; and whose soever sins ye retain, they are retained.

What do you believe in accordance with these words?

ANSWER: I believe that when the called ministers of Christ by His divine command deal with us, particularly when they exclude the manifest and impenitent sinners from the Christian congregation, and again absolve those who repent of their sins and are willing to amend — that this is as valid and certain, also in heaven, as if Christ our dear Lord had dealt with us Himself.

PART V

THE SACRAMENT OF THE ALTAR

I

What is the Sacrament of the Altar?

ANSWER: It is the true body and blood of our Lord Jesus Christ, under the bread and wine, given unto us Christians to eat and to drink, as it was instituted by Christ Himself.

Where is it so written?

ANSWER: The holy Evangelists, Matthew, Mark, and Luke, together with St. Paul, write thus:

"Our Lord Jesus Christ, in the night in which He was betrayed, took bread; and when He had given thanks, He brake it and gave it to His disciples, saying, Take, eat; this is My body, which is given for you; this do in remembrance of Me.

"After the same manner also He took the cup, when He had supped, and when He had given thanks, He gave it to them, saying, Drink ye all of it; this cup is the New Testament in My blood, which is shed for you, and for many, for the remission of sins; this do, as oft as ye drink it, in remembrance of Me."

II

What is the benefit of such eating and drinking?

ANSWER: It is pointed out in these words:

"Given and shed for you for the remission of sins."

Through these words the remission of sins, life and salvation are given unto us in the Sacrament; for where there is remission of sins, there is also life and salvation.

III

How can the bodily eating and drinking produce such
great benefits?

ANSWER: The eating and drinking, indeed, do not produce them, but the words:

"Given and shed for you for the remission of sins."

For besides the bodily eating and drinking, these words
are the chief thing in the Sacrament; and he who believes
them has what they say and declare, namely, the remission
of sins.

IV

Who, then, receives the Sacrament worthily?

ANSWER: Fasting and bodily preparation are indeed a
good outward discipline, but he is truly worthy and well
prepared who believes these words:

"Given and shed for you for the remission of sins."

But he who does not believe these words or who doubts
them, is unworthy and unprepared; for the words: "For
you," require truly believing hearts.

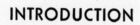

INTRODUCTION

LESSON 1

INTRODUCTION

1. Why do Christian people teach their children what to believe?

   a. Because God wants them to do so.

      Suffer (permit) the little children to come unto me. Mark 10:14.

   b. Because they want their children to be happy forever.

      Blessed are they that hear the Word of God and keep it. Luke 11:28.

   c. Because there are many false teachings in the world.

      Many false prophets are gone out into the world. I John 4:1.

2. What do Christians believe?

   What God has said in the Bible, which is His Word. (See NOTES, 1. Bible.)

   Thy Word is truth. John 17:17.

3. Who wrote the Bible?

   Men of God.

      Holy men of God spake as they were moved by the Holy Ghost. II Peter 1:21.

4. How can it be God's Word if men wrote it?

   God inspired them. (See NOTES, 2. Inspiration.)

> Which things also we speak, not in the
> words which man's wisdom teacheth, but which
> the Holy Ghost teacheth, comparing spiritual
> things with spiritual (combining spiritual things
> with spiritual words). I Cor. 2:13.

> All Scripture is given by inspiration of God.
> II Tim. 3:16.

5. Why do we study Luther's Catechism?

Because it truly sums up the main teachings
of the Bible. (See NOTES, 3. Dr. Martin
Luther.)

6. What is our catechism?

An explanation of Christian teaching.

7. What are the five chief parts of our catechism?

The Ten Commandments
The Christian Creed
The Lord's Prayer
Holy Baptism
The Lord's Supper

NOTES

1. THE BIBLE.

"The Bible" means "the Book." It is really a collection
of books or writings. These books were written at different
times by different men, from 1500 B. C. to 100 A. D.

The Bible is divided into two parts. The books that
were written before Christ came are called the Old Testament. There are 3 letters in "Old" and 9 letters in "Testament." Set these figures down side by side and you have
39. There are 39 books in the Old Testament.

The books that were written after Christ came are called
the New Testament. There are also 3 letters in "New" and

9 again in "Testament." This time multiply 3 times 9 and you have 27. There are 27 books in the New Testament. The whole Bible contains 39 plus 27 books, that is, 66. (A list of these 66 books may be found in the Appendix).

2. INSPIRATION.

To inspire means to "breathe in." When we say the Bible is inspired, we mean that God has breathed His Spirit into men, so that what they wrote was God's Word. Just how this was done, we are not able to say. But the men who wrote knew that what they wrote was of God, and said so. For example, in the Old Testament the prophet Jeremiah says, "The Word of the Lord came unto me" (Jer. 1:4). And in the New Testament the apostle Paul says, "The things that I write unto you are the commandments of the Lord" (I Cor. 14:37).

3. DR. MARTIN LUTHER.

Martin Luther lived about four hundred years ago, 1483-1546. He was a preacher and also a teacher in the university at Wittenberg, Germany.

While visiting the churches of Saxony (the part of Germany where he lived) he discovered how little the children and common people knew about the teachings of the Bible. So in 1529 he wrote his Small Catechism. It was to be used by parents and teachers in helping people, especially the young, to understand what the Bible teaches. That little book has been used by our Church for over four hundred years.

We are called "Lutherans" after Dr. Luther. It was a nickname at first, given by his enemies to those who followed Luther's teachings. Now we are proud of the name, for he was a great and good man, and taught the way of God in truth.

SCRIPTURE READING
Psalm 78:1-7

FOR CLASS DISCUSSION

Does it make any difference what people believe about
the multiplication table?
healthful habits for living?
religion?

Why not let children grow up and then decide for
themselves whether they want to learn about the Christian
religion? Do we let them decide for themselves whether
they will bathe, eat properly, be polite, go to school? Why
not?

Is there any difference between a Christian and a
Lutheran? Are all Christians Lutheran? Are all Lutherans
Christian?

PRAYER

Dear heavenly Father, I thank Thee for Thy Word.
Help me to learn what Thou hast told us of Thyself in
that Word. Bless all the members of our class, and our
teacher. In Jesus' name. Amen.

PART I

THE TEN COMMANDMENTS

MOSES RECEIVES THE TEN COMMANDMENTS

LESSON 2

THE TEN COMMANDMENTS

8. What are the Ten Commandments?

   They are the sum of God's holy law.

9. Why did God give us laws, or commandments?

   So that we might know what we ought to do,
   and what we ought not to do.

10. When did God give the Ten Commandments?

    He gave them through Moses to the children
    of Israel, about 1500 years before Christ.
    (See NOTES, 2. Giving of the Law.)

11. Was there no law of God before that?

    Yes, the law was written in men's hearts from
    creation. (See NOTES, 1. Conscience.)

    > For when the Gentiles, which have not the
    > law, do by nature the things contained in the
    > law, these, having not the law, are a law unto
    > themselves; which show the work of the law
    > written in their hearts, their conscience also
    > bearing witness. Rom. 2:14, 15.

12. What is the Introduction to the Ten Commandments?

    I am the Lord thy God.

13. Why does God begin His law with these words?

    To show us that He has the right to tell us
    what to do; for He is the Lord God who
    created the world.

14. How are the Ten Commandments divided?

    Into two parts, called tables. (See NOTES,
    3. The Two Tables.)

15.   Of what does the first table treat?

The first three commandments treat of love
to God.

> Thou shalt love the Lord thy God with all
> thy heart, and with all thy soul, and with all
> thy mind. Matthew 22:37.

16.   Of what does the second table treat?

The last seven commandments treat of love to
man.

> Thou shalt love thy neighbor as thyself.
> Matthew 22:39.

NOTES

1.   CONSCIENCE.

Conscience is the knowledge within ourselves that what
we do is right or wrong. When we do wrong we feel
guilty. We say that conscience accuses us. When we do
right we feel good about it. We say that conscience ap-
proves us. This still, small voice of conscience within us
shows the work of the law written in our hearts.

2.   GIVING OF THE LAW.

God gave the Ten Commandments through Moses to
the children of Israel. "Children of Israel" is the name
given to the Jewish people, the descendants of Abraham
(see John 8:33). Abraham's grandson, Jacob, was given
the name Israel by God (see Gen. 32:28). Jacob's sons
were the heads of the twelve tribes of Israel. They and
their families went down to Egypt to live. After four
hundred years those twelve families had become a great
people numbering two or three millions. God led them out
of Egypt under Moses, to bring them to the land He had
promised to Abraham, their ancestor. At one of the first
stops on the way, God called Moses up to the top of a

mountain (Mount Sinai), and gave him the law for the people.

3. The Two Tables.

In the book of Exodus, Moses himself writes about how he received the law from God. He says that he came down from the mountain with the two tables of the law (See Exodus 32:15, 16). In Ex. 34:1 we learn that they were "tables of stone." A table means a flat surface. Perhaps we would understand it better if we said "tablets" of stone. We are not told anywhere in the Bible how many commandments were on one table and how many on the other. But when Jesus was asked about the law, His answer spoke of two parts, love to God and love to our neighbor.

SCRIPTURE READING

Exodus 20:1-20

FOR CLASS DISCUSSION

Would you like to live in a home, or go to a school, or be a resident in a town where there were no rules or laws? Give reasons for your answer.

Give some law that the birds obey; the trees and flowers; the sun and moon. Were those laws passed by Congress? Whose laws are they?

Does conscience compel you to do right? What happens to conscience when its voice is not heeded?

PRAYER

Great God of heaven and earth, I thank Thee for Thy law. Help me to obey it, and help all men everywhere to obey it, that this world may be a happier place in which to live. This I ask in Jesus' name. Amen.

LESSON 3

THE FIRST COMMANDMENT

17. Which is the First Commandment?

    Thou shalt have no other gods before Me.

18. What does this mean?

    We should fear, love, and trust in God above all things.

19. What does this Commandment forbid?

    It forbids us to believe in or to serve any other gods but the one true God. (See NOTES, 1. God.)

    > I am the Lord, that is my name; and my glory will I not give to another, neither my praise to graven images. Isa. 42:8.

20. Are there any other gods?

    No, but people sometimes give their love and service to someone or something else than God. (See NOTES, 2. False Gods.)

21. Why is this wrong?

    Because the one true God who made us wants us to fear, love, and trust in Him above all things.

    > Thou shalt worship the Lord thy God, and Him only shalt thou serve. Matthew 4:10.

22. What does it mean to fear God above all things?

> It means to respect Him more than anything else.
>
> > **We ought to obey God rather than men. Acts 5:29.**

23. What does it mean to love God above all things?

> It means to find our highest pleasure and delight in Him. (See NOTES, 3. Fear and Love of God.)

24. What does it mean to trust in God above all things?

> It means to be sure that God and God only can take care of us at all times.

NOTES

1. GOD.

It should be clear to any thoughtful person that there is only one God. If there were more than one, there would be more than one will ruling the world. Then part of the stars might move in one direction and part in the opposite direction, and there would be collisions. Or the law of gravity might work to-day to keep you on the ground, and tomorrow a different law might cause you to fly up in the air. But no, the world operates in perfect order and harmony. This means that there is one will ruling it. That is, there is one God.

2. FALSE GODS.

False gods include any person or thing, real or imagined, to which men give the fear, love and trust which belong to God alone. Such false gods may be spirits, men, animals, or inanimate (non-living) objects.

a. **Spirits.** For example, the gods of the heathen. Sometimes they carve images or idols to represent these spirits. They often think of these gods as evil spirits, who will harm them if they do not offer gifts.

b. **Men.** If we respect men more than God, so that we would rather obey them than obey God, we sin against this Commandment.

If we love ourselves or someone else more than we love God, so that we would rather please ourselves or our friends than to please God, we sin against this Commandment.

If we trust in our own wisdom and strength, or in that of other men, rather than in God's all-wise and all-powerful care, we sin against this Commandment.

If we pray to saints (good people who have gone to heaven) rather than to God, we sin against this Commandment.

c. **Animals.** Some people have considered various animals sacred — the cow, the cat, the monkey, the crocodile — and have worshipped them.

d. **Things.** People have worshipped the sun or the moon. Today we know that these heavenly bodies are composed of the same kind of matter as our earth.

Other men, even to this day, think more of their money or other possessions than they do of God. This is making a false god of our possessions.

3. FEAR AND LOVE OF GOD.

This is all that God expects of us. That is why the words are repeated in the explanation of each commandment. If we do not fear and love God, He is not pleased with our obedience. The other commandments show how we should express the fear and love of God in every-day life.

SCRIPTURE READING
Isaiah 44:9-20

FOR CLASS DISCUSSION

What would you think of a man who would pick up a stone in his back yard and make a god of it? Would it make any difference if the stone were a diamond?

What can God do for you which no man can do? What can God supply you which no wealth could buy? Which is worth more to you, that which men can give or money can buy, or that which only God can give?

Suppose a man does not believe in any God. Does he sin against the First Commandment?

PRAYER

O God in heaven, Thou art the only true God. I will trust in Thee. Keep my heart as Thy possession, and let me love Thee above all things. Have mercy upon all people who worship false gods, and help them to love and serve Thee alone. Amen.

LESSON 4

THE SECOND COMMANDMENT

25. Which is the Second Commandment?

   Thou shalt not take the name of the Lord thy God in vain, for the Lord will not hold him guiltless that taketh His name in vain.

26. What does this mean?

   We should fear and love God so that we do not curse, swear, conjure, lie or deceive by His name, but call upon Him in every time of need, and worship Him with prayer, praise and thanksgiving.

27. What does this Commandment forbid?

   It forbids us to take God's name in vain, that is, to use God's name in foolish and sinful ways.

   > The Lord will not hold him guiltless that taketh His name in vain. Ex. 20:7.

28. What are some wrong uses of God's name?

   To curse, swear, conjure, lie or deceive by His name. (See NOTES, 1. Sins Against the Second Commandment.)

(34)

29. Are all these uses of God's name absolutely forbidden?

> They are all absolutely forbidden except swearing, that is, to take an oath. Taking an oath is permitted under certain circumstances. (See NOTES, 2. Oaths.)

>> Thou shalt fear the Lord thy God, and serve Him, and shalt swear by His name. Deut. 6:13.

30. What are some right uses of God's name?

> To call upon Him in every time of need, and worship Him with prayer, praise and thanksgiving.

>> Call upon me in the day of trouble; I will deliver thee, and thou shalt glorify me. Ps. 50:15.

31. What do we conclude from this Commandment?

> That the name of God is holy, and is to be used only in love and respect.

NOTES

1. SINS AGAINST THE SECOND COMMANDMENT.

   a. **Curse.** To curse God is to speak evil of Him (also called blasphemy). To curse men or animals or things is to wish evil to them by the name of God (for example, to ask God to damn someone). See Romans 12:14; James 3:8-10. "Dern," "darn," "dang," "ding," "dash," (why do they all begin with "d"?) are all substitutes for cursing.

   b. **Swear.** To swear is to call upon God to be a witness of the truth of what we say. See Leviticus 19:12; Leviticus 5:4; James 5:12; Matthew 5:34-37. "So help me God," is the form used in court. "By God" is an oath often used in conversation by people of unclean lips. "By gosh," "by gad," "by gee" (by G—), (why do they all begin with "g"?), "so help me," and "I hope to die" are substitutes for swearing.

   c. **Conjure.** To conjure by God's name is to pretend to be able to work magic, to call up the dead, to work charms and the like, by the use of His name. See Deuteronomy 18:10-12. Consulting mediums who claim to have a "familiar spirit" whom they call up from the dead (necromancy) is distinctly forbidden in this passage.

   d. **Lie or deceive.** To lie or deceive by God's name is to try to make people believe a lie is the truth by using God's name. Perjury in court (telling a lie when one has sworn to tell the truth) is lying by the name of God. Teaching false doctrine and claiming that it is God's Word is lying by the name of God. See Jeremiah 23:31, 32. Pretending to be a Christian, and then doing things that Christians should not do, is lying to the world in the name of God (hypocrisy). See Matthew 15:8.

2. Oaths.

Swearing needlessly or foolishly is forbidden. But we are to call upon God in every time of need. When someone is asked in court, "Do you solemnly swear that your testimony will be the truth, the whole truth, and nothing but the truth?" that may be considered a time of need. Our own need or our neighbor's need requires that judge and jury be sure that they have the truth, so that justice may be done. When Jesus was put on oath at His trial, He answered, so swearing in court must not be wrong. See Matthew 26:63, 64.

Other oaths that are permissible because they serve our neighbor's need are oaths of allegiance, taken by people who were born elsewhere but who wish to be citizens of our country; and oaths of office, taken by presidents, governors, judges, senators, and others.

Some God-fearing people refuse to take an oath at any time. The government respects their conscience and permits them to "affirm."

SCRIPTURE READING

I Samuel 28:3-20

FOR CLASS DISCUSSION

Would you like to have your name made fun of? Or your father's or mother's name? Suppose someone told a lie and said that the ruler of our country had told it; what would you think of that? Which is more important, the name of the ruler, or the name of God? Why?

What would be a good way to deal with people who take the name of God in vain —

have nothing more to do with them?
pretend that we did not hear?
ask them to respect a name that is dear to us?

We use the name of God in this class. Is that wrong? Why not?

PRAYER

I will praise Thee, my God, O King; and I will bless Thy name for ever and ever. Set a watch, O Lord, before my mouth; keep the door of my lips. Help me to love and respect Thy holy name, and never to use it wrongly. I ask it in Jesus' name. Amen.

LESSON 5

THE THIRD COMMANDMENT

32. Which is the Third Commandment?
    Remember the Sabbath day, to keep it holy.

33. What does this mean?
    We should fear and love God so that we do not despise His Word and the preaching of the same, but deem it holy, and gladly hear and learn it.

34. What does God require of us in this Commandment?
    That we keep holy the Lord's day, that is, use the Lord's day for hearing and learning His Word. (See NOTES, 1. The Sabbath, and 2. The Lord's Day.)

35. When is this done?
    a. When we do not let anything interfere with our going to church on Sunday.

    Not forsaking the assembling of ourselves together, as the manner of some is. Heb. 10:25.

    b. When we join with other Christians to build churches, train ministers, and in general see to it that there will be preaching of God's Word.

36. Is it enough to hear the Word of God?
    No, Christians not only hear it, but also do it; but there will be no doing of the Word unless it has first been heard.

    Be ye doers of the Word, and not hearers only, deceiving your own selves. James 1:22.

37.   Where should the Word of God be preached?

Wherever there are human beings to hear it.

> This Gospel of the kingdom shall be preached in all the world for a witness unto all nations. Matthew 24:14.
>
> How shall they believe in Him of whom they have not heard? and how shall they hear without a preacher? and how shall they preach except they be sent? Rom. 10:14, 15.

38.   What do we conclude from this Commandment?

That God wants us to make provision for the nourishment of our spiritual life. (See NOTES, 4. Family Worship.)

NOTES

1.   THE SABBATH.

Sabbath means "rest." The Jewish Sabbath was the seventh day of the week, or Saturday. See Exodus 20:9-11.

Some Christians still think that the seventh day of the week should be used for worship (Seventh Day Adventists, and others). But God tells us in the New Testament: "Let no man judge you in meat or in drink, or in respect of an holy day, or of the new moon, or of the Sabbath days" (Colossians 2:16). "Let no man judge you" means that the Christian is free in respect to such things.

2.   THE LORD'S DAY.

But the New Testament also says that we are not free from obedience to the Third Commandment, for we are not to forsake the assembling of ourselves together (Hebrews 10:25). How is it that Christians have come to use the first day of the week, Sunday, for that purpose?

The first Christians were all Jews, who had been trained from childhood to assemble in the synagogues on the Sabbath. They continued to do so. But they also had come to regard the first day of the week as sacred to the Lord. For Jesus had risen from the dead on that day. See Mark 16:2, ff. One week later, again on the first day of the week, He appeared to them again. See John 20:26. Seven weeks after Easter, again on the first day of the week, the Holy Spirit was poured out on the assembled believers. This day was called Pentecost, from a Greek word that means "the fiftieth." Pentecost Sunday is the fiftieth day, counting from Easter. See Acts 2:1. Also Leviticus 23:15, 16 (the day *after* the Sabbath).

Naturally they began to consider the first day of the week the Lord's day. They called it that. See Revelation 1:10. They came together for worship on that day. See Acts 20:7; I Corinthians 16:2. As long as the Christians were nearly all of Jewish birth they no doubt came together both on the Jewish Sabbath and on the Lord's day. But as the Gospel spread more and more among the Gentiles (non-Jewish people) who had never had synagogues and Sabbath day worship, the Lord's day was kept as the day for Christian worship, and the Sabbath was dropped.

3. Festival Days.

We also celebrate other days in the Church Year that do not fall on Sunday. These days commemorate some great thing that God has done for us. Christmas, which may come on any day of the week, commemorates the birth of Jesus, Good Friday the death of Jesus, Ascension Day, always Thursday, the ascending of Jesus to heaven. For a complete list of Sundays and festival days see Appendix, Church Year.

4. Family Worship.

Besides attending the public services of the congregation, Christians worship God privately in their own homes.

A Christian family will find some time during the day
when all its members can be together. At this regular time
every day family worship is held. This usually consists of
the reading of some portion of the Bible, and prayer. The
singing of a Christian hymn, the review of a part of the
catechism, or the study of a Sunday school lesson may also
be included.

SCRIPTURE READING
Matthew 12:1-13

FOR CLASS DISCUSSION

Is not Monday also the Lord's day? And the other
days of the week — are they not also the Lord's days?

Suppose you go to Sunday school and church on Sunday morning, but are so tired from a late Saturday night
that you cannot listen and worship; are you keeping the
Lord's Day holy? Suppose you are so excited about what
you plan to do on Sunday afternoon that you cannot pay
attention to God's Word; are you keeping the Lord's Day
holy?

What things do you think we should do or not do on
the Lord's Day? Sleep? Work? Play? Walk? Ride?
Buy and sell? Go to shows? Visit our friends? Visit the
sick? What should determine whether it is right or wrong
to do a certain thing on Sunday?

PRAYER

I thank Thee, Lord, that Thou dost care for my soul,
and dost feed it with the bread of life, Thy holy Word.
Make me hungry for that food, and satisfy my hunger,
lest my soul perish. Let Thy Gospel be preached among
us and in all the world, that men may believe and be saved
through Jesus Christ our Lord. Amen.

LESSON 6

THE FOURTH COMMANDMEN

39. Which is the Fourth Commandment?

Honor thy father and thy mother, t_ thy days may be long upon the land u ich the Lord thy God giveth thee.

40. What does this mean?

We should fear and love God so that we do not despise our parents and superiors, nor provoke them to anger, but honor, serve, obey, love, and esteem them.

41. What does God require of us in this Commandment?

That we honor our parents and superiors. (See Notes, 1. Christian Parents.)

42. When is this done?

When we think highly of those who are placed over us, do cheerfully what they ask us to do, and repay them with kindness and love for their care of us.

> Children, obey your parents in the Lord, for this is right. Eph. 6:1.
> Let them learn first to show piety at home, and to requite their parents, for that is good and acceptable before God. I Tim. 5:4.

43. What promise does God add to this Commandment?

That thy days may be long upon the land.

> Honor thy father and mother, which is the first commandment with promise; that it may be well with thee and thou mayest live long on the earth. Eph. 6:2, 3.

44. Who is included in the word "superiors"?

All those who are placed over us, such as teachers, employers, rulers. (See NOTES, 2. Superiors.)

> Servants, be subject to your masters. I Pet. 2:18.
> Put them in mind to be subject to principalities and powers, to obey magistrates. Titus 3:1.
> (Read Rom. 13:1-7.)

45. When, only, may we refuse to obey those placed over us?

When they command us to do what is sinful.

> We ought to obey God rather than men. Acts 5:29.

46. What does God require of those who are placed over others?

That they be worthy of love and respect.

NOTES

1. CHRISTIAN PARENTS.

One of the greatest blessings we can have is to be born in a Christian home and to have Christian parents. Such parents bring their children up "in the nurture and admonition of the Lord" (see Ephesians 6:4). That means that they train their children to be Christians, and set them the example of Christian living. When you were baptized, your parents (or sponsors) promised that they would see to it that you would be taught the Christian faith. They keep this promise by teaching you themselves at home, by taking you to Sunday school and church, and by sending you to confirmation class.

Sometimes when our parents are old or sick or poor we have the pleasure of taking care of them, and showing them kindness in return for all the kindness they have shown us.

2. SUPERIORS.

If the parents die when children are still young, some-one else must take the place of the parents. Step-parents, foster parents, grandparents, aunts and uncles, guardians, or others who thus take care of orphaned children, are to be honored the same as parents.

When your parents send you to school they expect you to obey the teacher. They have turned over to the teacher the duty of taking care of you for the time being. While you are in school the teacher is your "superior," that is, one placed over you. So also is the Sunday school teacher, and the pastor.

One of the Bible passages in the lesson says, "Servants, be subject to your masters." In our times we do not have slaves, and many of us are neither servants nor masters. But most of us either work for somebody or have some-body work for us. Those who work for others have the duty of honoring their employers (bosses, foremen, super-intendents, managers) by doing what they are asked to do, and doing it well. Employers also have the duty of being kind to those who work for them.

We also have rulers (superiors) in the state, or national government. The Bible says, "Honor the king" (I Peter 2:17). Some countries now have presidents instead of kings. We should respect those who have the leadership in our national affairs. Rulers also should look after the welfare of their people, and try to be worthy of honor.

SCRIPTURE READING

Ephesians 6:1-9

FOR CLASS DISCUSSION

How old is a child before he can walk? Before he can talk? Before he can fully take care of himself? Who takes care of him during those years? Why?

Could you earn a living for your family now? Would you be wise enough to be mayor of a city or governor of a state? How should we feel toward those who do these things for us?

When you grow up you will probably have children too. How can you show in your dealings with your children that you appreciate what your parents did for you?

PRAYER

Father in heaven, I thank Thee for Christian parents, and for teachers, pastors, judges and rulers who are placed over me to guide and help me. Teach me to honor and obey my parents and superiors, so that when I, myself, come to a position of authority, I may be a parent and superior who is worthy of the respect of those placed under me. In Jesus' name, Amen.

LESSON 7

THE FIFTH COMMANDMENT

47. Which is the Fifth Commandment?

    Thou shalt not kill.

48. What does this mean?

    *We should fear and love God so that we do
    our neighbor no bodily harm nor cause
    him any suffering, but help and befriend
    him in every need.*

49. What does God forbid in this Commandment?

    The taking of human life. (See NOTES, 1.
    Capital Punishment, 2. War.)

    > Whoso sheddeth man's blood, by man shall
    > his blood be shed. Gen. 9:6.

50. Why does Luther add that we should not do our
    neighbor any harm in his body?

    Murder begins with hatred in the heart. That
    hatred and anything which springs from
    it (such as insults, blows, injuries) is
    displeasing to God.

    > Whosoever hateth his brother is a murderer,
    > and ye know that no murderer hath eternal life
    > abiding in him. I John 3:15.
    > Out of the heart proceed evil thoughts, mur-
    > ders, etc. Matthew 15:19.

51. May one take his own life?

    No, suicide is also killing, and is forbidden.

52. What should we think of human life?

We should regard it as the creation of God, and therefore preserve and protect it wherever possible. (See Notes, 3. Helping Those in Need.)

53. What then does this Commandment require of us?

That we be kind and helpful to our neighbor, avoiding anything that might shorten or endanger his life. (See Notes, 4. Criminal Carelessness.)

> As we have therefore opportunity, let us do good unto all men. Gal. 6:10.
>
> Whatsoever ye would that men should do to you, do ye even so to them. Matthew 7:12.

54. To whom should we be kind and helpful?

To everyone; even our enemies.

> Love your enemies, do good to them which hate you, bless them that curse you, and pray for them which despitefully use you. Luke 6:27, 28.

NOTES

1. Capital Punishment.

Capital punishment means punishment by death. When God said, "Whoso sheddeth man's blood, by man shall his blood be shed" (Genesis 9:6), He laid down a rule that permits capital punishment. Of course that does not mean that anyone who pleases may put a criminal to death. The government does it through its courts and law officers. When the government punishes a criminal with death, it acts as the agent or servant of God. Read Romans 13:1-4, and note the words, "He beareth not the sword in vain," and "He is the minister (servant) of God." (Some of our states do not have capital punishment.)

2. WAR.

Many people have been killed in wars. To hate whole nations is certainly no more pleasing to God than to hate one person. Only when nations act like criminals — when they invade our land and kill our people — are we right in fighting them. If your life were threatened by an insane person, you might protect your life by injuring the attacker. The law would not hold you guilty; that is self-defense. Nations, too, may fight in self-defense.

3. HELPING THOSE IN NEED.

Luther says we should help and befriend our neighbor in every need. That is the meaning of this commandment of God. We do this as citizens when we pay taxes, from which the poor, the aged and the sick are supported and helped; also when we subscribe to community funds, join the Red Cross and the like. We do it as Christians when we help support the Church's works of mercy; orphans' homes, old folks' homes, hospitals, inner missions.

4. CRIMINAL CARELESSNESS.

One may endanger the lives of other people by doing nothing. If you discovered a broken rail on a railroad and did not report it, you would be partly to blame for any wreck that occurred there.

It is still worse to endanger other people by our carelessness. Some cities have a law that when sidewalks are icy the property owners must sprinkle ashes or sand on them to save people from injury. Why are red lanterns placed on obstructions in the road?

To go among other people when one is suffering from a contagious disease is a criminal act. (Explain "quarantine".)

More people have been killed by automobiles in this country than have been killed in all our wars. To drive when one is not able to control the machine properly, or to drive recklessly or at too high a rate of speed is dangerous to human life, and is a sin against God's law as well as man's.

SCRIPTURE READING

Luke 10:25-37

FOR CLASS DISCUSSION

If I plant a seed and an apple tree comes up, what kind of seed did I plant? Could it not have been a peach seed? Why not? If I have an apple tree, what kind of fruit will it bear? Seed, tree, and fruit are all apple.

Hatred is a seed and murder is its fruit. If we allow the seed of murder to grow in our hearts, what kind of fruit will it produce? If the fruit is murder, what is the seed?

Another form of murder that grows out of the same seed of hate is hateful words. How could hateful words hurt anyone? Could they make him ill? Could they shorten his life? Would that be murder?

PRAYER

O God, I thank Thee for the precious gift of life. As I value my own life, health and happiness, so let me value and protect the life, health and happiness of others. So will I love my neighbor as myself. Amen.

LESSON 8

THE SIXTH COMMANDMENT

55. Which is the Sixth Commandment?

Thou shalt not commit adultery.

56. What does this mean?

We should fear and love God so that we lead a chaste and pure life in word and deed, and that husband and wife love and honor each other.

57. What does God require in this Commandment?

That we honor marriage, which was instituted by God; and therefore avoid all sins against this estate, either before or during our married life. (See NOTES, 1. Marriage.)

> Marriage is honorable in all. Heb. 13:4.
> What God hath joined together, let not man put asunder. Matthew 19:6.

58. For what purpose did God institute marriage?

In order that man and wife might establish a godly home and rear children in the fear and love of God.

59. Who sins against this Commandment?

1. He who is unfaithful to his own marriage partner or causes another to be unfaithful. (See NOTES, 2. Divorce.)

> Whosoever shall put away his wife, except it
> be for fornication, and shall marry another,
> committeth adultery. Matthew 19:9.

2. He who marries someone he has no right to marry.

> It is reported commonly that there is forni-
> cation among you, and such fornication as is not
> so much as named among the Gentiles, that one
> should have his father's wife. I Cor. 5:1.

3. He who is impure in thought, word and deed.

> Whosoever looketh on a woman to lust after
> her hath committed adultery with her already in
> his heart. Matthew 5:28. (Adultery in thought.)

60. Why are we told to be pure even in thought and word?

Because all sins begin in the heart, and unclean deeds are the product of a heart
that has learned to love uncleanness.

> Out of the heart proceed evil thoughts,
> murders, adulteries, fornications, thefts, false
> witness, blasphemies. Matthew 15:19.
> Blessed are the pure in heart, for they shall
> see God. Matthew 5:8.

61. How may young people prepare for a happy married life?

By keeping their bodies clean and strong and
their thoughts pure. (See Notes, 3.
Purity in Youth.)

> Keep thyself pure. I Tim. 5:22.
> Flee fornication. I Cor. 6:18.

NOTES

1. MARRIAGE.

Marriage is the life-long union of one man and one woman as husband and wife. God instituted marriage in Eden when He made Eve to be Adam's helpmeet. The family is the foundation of society; both the Church and the State are composed of people who are members of families. Neither the Church nor the State can prosper if the basic unit, the family, is weak and unstable; that is, if husband and wife do not love and honor each other, hold the family together, and train the children to be God-fearing people and honorable citizens. A large proportion of the children and young people who get into trouble and appear in the courts are found to be the children of parents who are separated. Obedience to the Sixth Commandment lies at the very root of all human relationships.

2. DIVORCE.

Jesus recognizes only one reason for divorce. If one of the married persons has sinned grievously against the Sixth Commandment, the other may apply to the court for a divorce. When divorced, the innocent one may in time remarry. Matthew 19:3-9.

St. Paul mentions another case. If one of the married persons runs away (deserts), and refuses to return, then the one who is left is not required to remain unmarried for life. He or she may go into court after a period of years and have the former marriage declared void because of the absence of the missing one. The cases are not the same. Jesus mentions the one case where a married person *may take steps to obtain a divorce*. Paul describes the case of one who has *unwillingly suffered* a separation through the desertion of the other. I Cor. 7:15.

Lutheran pastors will not remarry persons who have been separated for other reasons than those given above.

3. PURITY IN YOUTH.

Youth is a time of temptation to sins of the flesh. That young people may come to their marriage with sound bodies and clean hearts, it is important that they avoid these sins. Christian young people will not associate with persons of unclean lips; will not read stories or go to motion pictures or plays which present unclean ideas; will avoid indecent exposure of their bodies, also all games or practices which form a temptation to themselves or others. Keep thyself pure.

SCRIPTURE READING
Ephesians 5:22-33

FOR CLASS DISCUSSION

What do you think we Christians could do about motion picture plays in which the hero or heroine falls in love with someone else's wife or husband? Are such plays or stories harmful? Isn't it just play-acting? Is there anything we can do about it?

Read Proverbs 23:7, Matthew 15:19, Proverbs 4:23, Romans 12:9, Philippians 4:8. From these passages it is clear that we should guard our inmost thoughts from impurity. Does that mean that we should stay away from motion pictures altogether?

Would it be better to withdraw from the world and not marry at all, like monks and nuns? What did Jesus think about this? Read John 17:15-17.

PRAYER

Holy Father in heaven, when I am tempted to impure thoughts, words or deeds, help me to remember this word: How can I do this great wickedness and sin against God? Amen.

LESSON 9

THE SEVENTH COMMANDMENT

62. Which is the Seventh Commandment?

Thou shalt not steal.

63. What does this mean?

We should fear and love God so that we do not rob our neighbor of his money or property, nor bring them into our possession by unfair dealing or fraud, but help him to improve and protect his property and living.

64. What does God forbid in this Commandment?

He forbids stealing, that is, taking something which does not belong to us. (See NOTES, 1. Stealing.)

Let him that stole, steal no more. Eph. 4:28.

65. What is meant by "unfair dealing or fraud"?

It means cheating, or failing to give our neighbor a fair return for what we get from him. (See NOTES, 2. Cheating.)

Woe unto him that buildeth his house by unrighteousness, and his chambers by wrong; that useth his neighbor's service without wages, and giveth him not for his work. Jer. 22:13.

If any would not work, neither should he eat. II Thes. 3:10.

66. What does this Commandment require of us?

That we help our neighbor to improve and protect his property and living.

> If thou meet thine enemy's ox or his ass going astray, thou shalt surely bring it back to him again. Ex. 23:4.

67. To whom do all things belong?

All things belong to God.

> The earth is the Lord's and the fulness thereof; the world and they that dwell therein. Ps. 24:1.

68. What is therefore the right use of wealth?

We should use it in ways that are pleasing to God. (See NOTES, 3. Stewardship.)

> Whoso hath this world's good, and seeth his brother have need, and shutteth up his bowels of compassion from him, how dwelleth the love of God in him? I John 3:17.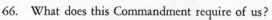

NOTES

1. STEALING.

Stealing is called "robbery" when it is done openly and by force; "theft" when it is done secretly and by stealth: "burglary" when it is done by breaking into a house; "embezzlement" when it means taking money that passes through our hands but belongs to others. All stealing is forbidden both by the law of God and of man.

If we find something of value, we should make an effort to discover its true owner, and return it to him.

2. CHEATING.

There are many forms of cheating, that is, getting something of value without giving a fair return. Here are some of the sins we should avoid:

Using false weights and measures.

Paying employes less than their labor is worth.

Taking pay for work that is not honestly done.

Selling something of no value.

Taking advantage of our neighbor's ignorance of the value of what he has.

Borrowing without expecting to pay back.

Charging too high a rate of interest (usury).

Gambling. All gamblers hope to get something for nothing. Betting on contests and games, playing slot-machines, selling chances, taking part in raffles and lotteries are forms of gambling.

3. STEWARDSHIP.

A steward is one who is in charge of someone else's property. Stewards are responsible to the person whose property they manage. "It is required in stewards that a man be found faithful" (I Cor. 4:2). "Give an account of thy stewardship" (Luke 16:2).

Since all wealth is God's we are all stewards. We must answer to God for the way we have managed that portion of His wealth which He entrusted to us.

We must not waste it. When Jesus fed five thousand men with a few loaves and fishes, He said, "Gather up the fragments that remain, that nothing be lost" (John 6:12). To waste or destroy food that hungry people would be glad to have, to destroy valuable property (as in strikes or war) is not good stewardship.

We must use it as God would like to have it used. To share with others, to feed the hungry and clothe the naked, to care for the sick and the suffering, to send God's Word to those who do not have it; these are uses of wealth which are pleasing to God. "To do good and to communicate (share) forget not; for with such sacrifices God is well pleased" (Hebrews 13:16). "God loveth a cheerful giver" (II Corinthians 9:7).

SCRIPTURE READING

Luke 19:1-10

FOR CLASS DISCUSSION

Is it a sin to be rich? Read Matthew 19:23-26. What does Jesus say about riches and heaven? But read also Genesis 13:2 and Luke 16:22. Is it dangerous to be rich? Read Matthew 6:19-21 and v. 24. What is the danger? See Proverbs 30:8, 9.

If a man is responsible for the way he gets wealth, is he also responsible for the way he spends it? Who has more responsibility before God, a rich man or a poor man?

Why are stealing and cheating not good ways in which to get wealth? Can you think of some ways in which one might honestly grow wealthy?

PRAYER

Dear God, let me never try to take that which belongs to another. Help me to be content with that portion of Thy wealth which Thou dost commit to my keeping, and to use it in a manner pleasing to Thee. Amen.

LESSON 10

THE EIGHTH COMMANDMENT

69. Which is the Eighth Commandment?

Thou shalt not bear false witness against thy neighbor.

70. What does this mean?

We should fear and love God so that we do not deceitfully belie, betray, backbite, nor slander our neighbor, but apologize for him, speak well of him, and put the most charitable construction on all that he does.

71. What does God forbid in this Commandment?

He forbids us to bear false witness, that is, to belie, betray, backbite or slander our neighbor. (See NOTES, 1. Sins Against the Eighth Commandment.)

> Speak not evil, one of another. James 4:11.
> A false witness shall not be unpunished, and he that speaketh lies shall not escape. Prov. 19:5.

72. Does this refer only to false witness in court?

No, we are not to bear false witness at any time. (See NOTES, 3. Lying in Business, 4. Society, 5. Politics.)

> Putting away lying, speak every man truth with his neighbor, for we are members one of another. Eph. 4:25.

(58)

73. Is lying always wrong?

> Yes; God is truth and lying is of the evil one. If we fear and love God, we shall hate and despise lying.
>
>> He (Satan) is a liar, and the father of it. John 8:44.
>> All liars shall have their part in the lake which burneth with fire and brimstone. Rev. 21:8.

74. What does the Eighth Commandment require of us?

> We should apologize for our neighbor (excuse and defend him).
>
> We should speak well of him.
>
> We should put the most charitable construction on all that he does (explain it in the kindest way). (See NOTES, 2. Gossip.)
>
>> Open thy mouth for the dumb in the cause of all such as are appointed to destruction. Open thy mouth, judge righteously, and plead the cause of the poor and needy. Prov. 31:8, 9.
>> Love . . . beareth all things, believeth all things, hopeth all things, endureth all things. I Cor. 13:7.

NOTES

1. SINS AGAINST THE EIGHTH COMMANDMENT.

   a. **Bearing false witness.** This may occur in court. (See Second Commandment, Notes 1, b, d, and 2.) In a wider sense all lying is false witness.

   b. **Belie,** to lie about.

   c. **Betray,** to reveal secrets which it is not our business to reveal. Only if others are endangered by our keeping still should we reveal secrets.

d. **Backbite,** to speak evil of someone behind his back.

e. **Slander,** to give someone a bad reputation by our evil and untrue statements.

(Other things mentioned below are also sins against the Eighth Commandment, though not named in the Commandment or its explanation.)

2. GOSSIP.

Gossip is idle talk, the spreading of ill-grounded rumors, especially of scandalous reports. We should not even lend our ears to it.

3. LYING IN BUSINESS.

Business men are coming to see more and more the value of truth in advertising and in all business dealings. Occasionally one mistakenly thinks that he can profit by misrepresenting goods, by deceiving customers, or by slandering competitors.

4. LYING IN SOCIETY.

People sometimes think that "harmless" lying as a social custom is excusable: as to pay compliments that are not sincere, or to give untruthful excuses for not doing something expected. "Your playing was marvelous" (when one doesn't really think so). "Mrs. A. has a headache and cannot see you" (when Mrs. A. just doesn't want to see the caller). In the long run people will respect us more if they know we are always truthful and sincere, without, of course, being rude.

5. LYING IN POLITICS.

This is very common. Candidates for office put the worst construction on what their opponents say or do, speakers slander the other party, office-holders deceive the public.

In international politics lying propaganda is used, treaties are signed and then disregarded. Nations cannot long prosper by such means. "Righteousness exalteth a nation, but sin is a reproach to any people." Proverbs 14:34.

SCRIPTURE READING

John 8:37-47

FOR CLASS DISCUSSION

If, instead of harming your neighbor, you could help him by telling a lie, would that be right? Who is the father of lies? Whose children are we? Can we serve God by serving the devil? Can we do evil that good may come? Romans 3:7, 8.

When would it be right to "tell on" some one?

Are fairy tales and other fiction stories lies? If not, why not?

Many years ago a man stole some money and served a term in prison. Since then he has become a Christian, has moved to a different state, has married, is the father of fine and respected children, has a position of trust and responsibility. Suppose I go to his employer and say, "You have a thief working for you." Would that be the truth or a lie?

PRAYER

Set a watch, O Lord, before my mouth; keep the door of my lips (Ps. 141:3). Help me always to speak the truth in love, for Thou art truth and I am Thy child through Jesus Christ, my Savior. Amen.

LESSON 11

THE NINTH COMMANDMENT

75. Which is the Ninth Commandment?

Thou shalt not covet thy neighbor's house.

76. What does this mean?

We should fear and love God so that we do not seek by craftiness to gain possession of our neighbor's inheritance or home, nor obtain them under pretense of a legal right, but assist and serve him in keeping the same.

77. What does it mean to covet?

It means to desire wrongfully. (See NOTES, 1. Covetousness and Kindred Sins.)

> But godliness with contentment is great gain. For we brought nothing into this world, and it is certain we can carry nothing out. And having food and raiment let us be therewith content. I Tim. 6:6, 8.

78. What then does the Ninth Commandment forbid?

It forbids the wrongful desire to obtain our neighbor's house or inheritance.

> Woe unto you, scribes and Pharisees, hypocrites! for ye devour widows' houses, and for a pretense make long prayer; therefore ye shall receive the greater damnation. Matthew 23:14.

(62)

79. Is it always wrong to desire our neighbor's property?

No, not if he is willing to dispose of his property, and we offer him fair value for it.

80. What does it mean to obtain our neighbor's property under pretense of a legal right?

It means to take it away from him by some trick of the law. (See NOTES, 2. Pretense of Legal Right.)

81. What does the Ninth Commandment require?

That we assist and serve our neighbor in keeping his property.

> Look not every man on his own things, but every man also on the things of others. Phil. 2:4. By love serve one another. Gal. 5:13.

NOTES

1. COVETOUSNESS AND KINDRED SINS.

"Covet" once meant simply "desire." The word is so used in the Bible. "Covet earnestly the best gifts" (I Cor. 12:31). Now it is used almost always in a bad sense, to desire wrongfully. It may be a sinful desire either because we desire something we ought not to have at all, or because our desire is so strong that we would be willing to do wrong to get what we want.

The one who covets his neighbor's possessions is also *envious*. To envy another is to wish that one had his wealth, honor, position, power, friends, or anything of value.

The covetous person is quite likely to be *greedy* also. A greedy person wants more than his share of everything, more than one person should have or can use.

One who is covetous of wealth may also become *avaricious,* that is, grasping and miserly, always wanting to get and never to give.

2. PRETENSE OF LEGAL RIGHT.

By obtaining possession of our neighbor's property under pretense of a legal right we mean getting it away from him in such a way that the law of man does not punish the act, even though the higher law of God condemns it.   Examples:

Getting someone to sign a paper which he has not fully examined, and thus sign away his rights or possessions.

Taking advantage of a man's ignorance of the value of his property.

Persuading a man's creditors to press for payment and thus throw him into bankruptcy, so that we may buy his property cheaply in a forced sale.

Buying the mortgage on the home of poor people with the thought in mind of foreclosing the mortgage at the first opportunity, and thus taking the home away from them.

SCRIPTURE READING

I Kings 21:1-19

FOR CLASS DISCUSSION

Suppose my neighbor has many friends, a good disposition, a good education. Is it wrong for me to wish that I had friends, kindliness, learning? Can I get them by wishing for them? What should I do?

Is it wrong for a poor man to wish that his family had a better house, better clothes, better food? What should he do about it? Would it be right for him to want to get them for his family by taking them away from some other family?

What is the golden rule that governs all our dealings with our neighbor? See Matthew 7:12.

PRAYER

Father, I thank Thee that Thou hast given me many good things, and I know that Thou wilt care for me always. Let me never desire anything but that which it is Thy will for me to have. Keep my heart from covetousness and envy. Amen.

LESSON 12

THE TENTH COMMANDMENT

82. Which is the Tenth Commandment?

Thou shalt not covet thy neighbor's wife, nor his manservant, nor his maidservant, nor his cattle, nor anything that is thy neighbor's.

83. What does this mean?

We should fear and love God so that we do not estrange or entice away our neighbor's wife, servants, or cattle, but seek to have them remain and discharge their duty to him. (See NOTES, 1. Sins Against the Tenth Commandment.)

84. What does the Tenth Commandment forbid?

It also forbids coveting, or evil desire.

> Every man is tempted when he is drawn away of his own lust (evil desire) and enticed. James 1:14.

85. Why does God add this Commandment to the others?

To show that *all* evil desires are sinful.

86. Where do these evil desires come from?

We are born with them. (See NOTES, 2. Original Sin.)

> We all . . . . were by nature (by birth) the children of wrath, even as others. Eph. 2:3.
> That which is born of the flesh is flesh. John 3:6.

(66)

87. If we yield to these evil desires, what is the result?
> The result is sinful acts. (See NOTES, 3.
> Actual Sin.)
> > Out of the heart proceed evil thoughts, mur-
> > ders, adulteries, fornications, thefts, false wit-
> > ness, blasphemies. Matthew 15:19.

88. What then does this Commandment require?
> That we subdue our evil desires, or that we
> be pure in thought, word and deed.
> > Ye shall be holy; for I, the Lord your God,
> > am holy. Lev. 19:2.

89. What should move us to such holiness of life?
> The fear and love of God.

NOTES

1. SINS AGAINST THE TENTH COMMANDMENT.

To *estrange* means to make strange, to alienate. When someone comes between husband and wife and causes trouble between them, so that they no longer love each other but are strangers to one another, he has estranged them.

To *entice* means to lead away by promises. A man's servant may be enticed by promises of better pay. In strikes it has happened that workmen who wanted to stay and work were driven away by threats of bodily harm.

To entice a public servant or officer of the government from doing his duty by giving him money is called *bribery,* and is punished severely.

2. ORIGINAL SIN.

Original sin is the sin that is in the whole human race since our first parents disobeyed God. "As by one man sin entered into the world, and death by sin; and so death passed upon all men, for that all have sinned." Romans 5:12.

3. ACTUAL SIN.

"Actual" as here used does not mean "real," so that this would be considered real sin, but not the other. Original sin is real sin, too. But actual sin means sins in acts.

And by acts we do not mean only something that is done with the hands or feet. Our words are also our acts. Even our thoughts, if we willingly yield to temptation and think of doing evil things, are acts.

SCRIPTURE READING
Philemon

FOR CLASS DISCUSSION

The Tenth Commandment does not mention children. Can children also be estranged from their parents? Can they be enticed away from their duty? Name some ways children are enticed.

Would it ever be right to offer another man's workman more money if he will work for you? But suppose the other man's crop would be lost if his workman leaves. Or if the workman is a salesman, suppose he takes all the other man's customers over to you. It is plain that sometimes it would be wrong. Can you formulate a rule that tells when it is wrong?

PRAYER

O God, Thou faithful God,
   Thou Fountain ever flowing,
Who all we need in life
   In mercy art bestowing:
Give me a healthy frame,
   And may I have within
A conscience free from blame,
   A soul unhurt by sin. Amen.

LESSON 13

THE CONCLUSION

90. What does God declare concerning all these Commandments?

He says: I the Lord thy God am a jealous God, visiting the iniquity of the fathers upon the children unto the third and fourth generation of them that hate Me; and showing mercy unto thousands of them that love Me and keep My commandments. (See NOTES, 1. The Conclusion.)

91. What does this mean?

God threatens to punish all who transgress these commandments. We should therefore fear His wrath, and in no wise disobey them. But He promises grace and every blessing to all who keep them. We should therefore love Him, trust in Him, and gladly keep His commandments.

92. What is God's attitude to sin?

He hates sin and punishes it. (See NOTES, 2. Sin, 3. Punishment of Sin.)

The wages of sin is death. Rom. 6:23.

(69)

93. What should we therefore do?

> We should therefore fear His wrath and in no wise disobey His commandments.

94. What does God promise to all who keep His commandments?

> He promises grace and every blessing to all who keep them. (See NOTES, 4. Grace.)

95. What should we therefore do?

> We should therefore love Him, trust in Him, and gladly keep His commandments.

96. Does anyone keep the commandments of God perfectly?

> No, we are all sinners.

>> If we say that we have no sin, we deceive ourselves and the truth is not in us. I John 1:8.

97. Of what use then is the Law of God?

> a. It shows us our sins and our need of a Savior.
>
> b. It shows us what we ought to do to be pleasing to God.

98. Since we are sinners, what do we need?

> We need the forgiveness which God gives us for Jesus' sake.

>> God . . . hath made Him to be sin for us who knew no sin, that we might be made the righteousness of God in Him. II Cor. 5:21.
>>
>> The wages of sin is death; but the gift of God is eternal life through Jesus Christ our Lord. Rom. 6:23.

NOTES

1. The Conclusion.

A jealous God. When we are jealous it means that we are afraid someone else is taking our place, is getting the love or respect or honor that belongs to us. We do not like that. God is jealous in the sense that He is greatly displeased when men do not give Him the love, respect and honor that is due Him.

Visiting iniquity. Iniquity is sin, evil-doing. We usually think of "visiting" our friends. God does not visit iniquity as a friend, for He hates sin. When He visits iniquity it is for the same reason that a policeman comes to see a law-breaker — to bring the punishment of the law. Therefore Luther says, "God threatens to punish."

Unto the third and fourth generation. That means that not only the children of sinners, but sometimes even the grandchildren and great-grandchildren have to suffer with them. Weaknesses of body or mind may be inherited, loss of property or position may have to be borne for generations. It does not mean that God holds anyone guilty for someone else's sin. See Ezekiel 18:20.

2. Sin.

Sin is called in the Conclusion "iniquity" and "hating God," and in Luther's explanation it is called "transgressing the commandments" and "disobeying the commandments." All these expressions mean going contrary to God's will.

3. Punishment of Sin.

The whole human race suffers as a consequence of sin. All sickness, pain, sorrow and death have come into the world as the result of sin. Jesus teaches us however that we are not to think of each separate sorrow as the punishment for some particular sin. See John 9:1-3. The punishment of sin will continue in eternity if it is not forgiven.

4. GRACE.

God promises grace to all who keep His commandments. Grace here means kindness, goodness, mercy, help, blessing. See John 8:31, 32. John 14:23.

SCRIPTURE READING

Jonah 3

FOR CLASS DISCUSSION

When a criminal is sent to prison or is executed, the newspapers reporting the case often say, "Crime does not pay." What does that mean? If crime does not pay when it is man's law that is broken, do you think it will "pay" to break God's law? What does this mean, "The wages of sin is death"?

Does God have policemen watching us to enforce His law? Isn't it rather easy then for us to evade the law of God? Is it easier to escape the consequences when we break man's law or when we break God's law? Can you name some of the ways God has of enforcing His law?

PRAYER

O God, we thank Thee for Thy law which tells us how we ought to live. Help us to keep Thy commandments, and where we fail and come short, forgive us for Jesus' sake. Amen.

PART II

THE CREED

CREATION

LESSON 14

INTRODUCTION

99. Repeat the Apostles' Creed.

I believe in God the Father Almighty, Maker of heaven and earth; and in Jesus Christ, His only Son, our Lord; who was conceived by the Holy Ghost, born of the Virgin Mary; suffered under Pontius Pilate, was crucified, dead, and buried; He descended into hell; the third day He rose again from the dead; He ascended into heaven, and sitteth on the right hand of God the Father Almighty, from thence He shall come to judge the quick and the dead. I believe in the Holy Ghost; the holy Christian Church, the communion of saints; the forgiveness of sins; the resurrection of the body; and the life everlasting. Amen.

100. What is the Apostles' Creed?

It is a short statement of what Christians believe. (See NOTES, 1. The Three Christian Creeds.)

> With the heart man believeth unto righteousness; and with the mouth confession is made unto salvation. Rom. 10:10.

101. In whom do Christians believe?

> They believe in the one true God: Father, Son and Holy Ghost. (See NOTES, 2. The Triune God.)

>> Go ye therefore and teach all nations, baptizing them in the name of the Father, and of the Son, and of the Holy Ghost. Matthew 28:19.
>> The grace of the Lord Jesus Christ, and the love of God, and the communion of the Holy Ghost be with you all. II Cor. 13:14.

102. How does the Bible describe God?

> The Bible describes God as a Spirit, who is eternal, almighty, all-wise, omnipresent, holy, righteous, merciful and truthful. (See NOTES, 3. Law and Gospel.)

>> God is a spirit. John 4:24.
>> From everlasting to everlasting Thou art God. Ps. 90:2.
>> With God nothing shall be impossible. Luke 1:37.
>> Lord, Thou knowest all things. John 21:17.
>> Do not I fill heaven and earth? saith the Lord. Jer. 23:24.
>> I, the Lord your God, am holy. Lev. 19:2.
>> The Lord our God is righteous in all His works. Dan. 9:14.
>> The Lord is merciful and gracious. Ps. 103:8.
>> All His works are done in truth. Ps. 33:4.

NOTES

1. THE THREE CHRISTIAN CREEDS.

There are three Christian confessions of faith which are ecumenical, that is, which belong to all Christians everywhere. (Different Christian denominations also have confessions which belong to them only; for example, Luther's Catechism is a Lutheran confession.) The three ecumenical creeds are the Apostles' Creed, the Nicene Creed, and the Athanasian Creed.

a. **The Apostles' Creed.** This is the Creed explained in the Catechism. It was not written by the apostles, but it contains a summary of what the apostles taught.

b. **The Nicene Creed.** This creed was adopted by the Christian Church in the fourth century.

c. **The Athanasian Creed.** This creed probably originated in the Church about 500 A. D. Its purpose is to emphasize the Christian doctrine of the Trinity. It was named after Athanasius, a Christian bishop (died 373 A. D.).

2. THE TRIUNE GOD.

The Bible teaches that there is one God, but three Persons; Father, Son, and Holy Ghost (Spirit). We therefore speak of the triune (three-one) God, and of the doctrine of the Trinity (three-oneness). We do not understand this; we simply take God's word for it, because He so reveals Himself. All true Christians believe in the Trinity. They are Trinitarian.

3. LAW AND GOSPEL.

Describing God we say that He is holy, righteous, merciful and truthful.

He is holy because He loves good and hates evil; and He is righteous because He rewards good and punishes evil. As the holy and righteous God He has given us His Law which we must obey. We have seen (Lesson 13) that we are all sinners and do not perfectly keep God's holy Law.

Therefore we rejoice that He is also merciful and truthful. Because He is merciful He has provided for us in Christ Jesus a way of salvation from our sins; and because He is truthful we know that we can rely on the Gospel, which tells us of that way of salvation.

The Law is every word of God that condemns sin. The Gospel is every word of God that offers forgiveness of sin through Christ.

In the Creed we confess our faith in the great deeds of God for our salvation.

SCRIPTURE READING

I Kings 18

FOR CLASS DISCUSSION

When Christopher Columbus sailed west across the Atlantic Ocean, did he believe that he would find land? Had he ever seen that land? Do you believe in things you have not seen? Have you ever seen Japan? Has anyone ever seen conscience, love, kindness, patriotism? (We see the evidences of these qualities, but not the qualities themselves.) These are soul qualities, spiritual qualities. Is a rock patriotic? Can a tree love? Only souls (or spirits) can have spiritual qualities. Is the soul visible? Do you believe that you are a soul? Why? Is it any more difficult to believe in the great Spirit, God, than to believe in the spirit within you, your own soul? Read Hebrews 11:1 for a definition of faith.

PRAYER

Triune God, Father, Son and Holy Spirit, I thank Thee for Thy great love toward me. Speak to me in Thy Word, and strengthen the faith of Thy child, and my love to Thee. Amen.

LESSON 15

THE FIRST ARTICLE, OF CREATION

103. Which is the First Article of the Creed?

I believe in God the Father Almighty, maker of heaven and earth.

104. What does this mean?

I believe that God has created me and all that exists; that He has given and still preserves to me my body and soul, my eyes and ears, and all my members, my reason and all the powers of my soul, together with food and raiment, home and family, and all my property; that He daily provides abundantly for all the needs of my life, protects me from all danger, and guards and keeps me from all evil; and that He does this purely out of fatherly and divine goodness and mercy, without any merit or worthiness in me; for all which I am in duty bound to thank, praise, serve, and obey Him. This is most certainly true.

105. Of whom does the First Article treat?

Of God the Father, my Creator.

106. What did God create?

I believe that God has created me and all that exists. (See NOTES, 1. Creation, and 2. Theory of Evolution.)

In the beginning God created the heaven and the earth. Gen. 1:1.

(79)

107.   What has God given you?

     a. My body, with all its members.

     b. By soul, with all its powers. (See NOTES, 3. Body and Soul.)

> The Spirit of God hath made me, and the breath of the Almighty hath given me life. Job 33:4.

108.   For what purpose did God create men?

That He might love us, and that we in turn might love Him.

> God is love. I John 4:16.
> Thou shalt love the Lord thy God. Matthew 22:37.

NOTES

1.   CREATION.

I believe that God has created all that exists. To create means to bring into being that which did not formerly exist. God has brought all things into being.

That includes the world of inanimate things (things without life) such as the heavenly bodies, the sun and the stars, the earth and the other planets that revolve around the sun. It includes all forms of plant life and animal life on the earth.

It includes also the highest form of life on the earth, man. Man differs from all other forms of life on the earth because he is a living soul. "God breathed into his nostrils the breath of life and man became a living soul" (Genesis 2:7). That is, man is both material (the body) and spiritual (the soul). God is a spirit, and He made man to be like Himself. "God created man in His own image." Genesis 1:26, 27). Man was like God in goodness.

The angels are also spiritual beings created by God. The Bible tells us that some of the angels have become evil and are God's enemies. The good angels do God's will. (Thy will be done on earth as it is in heaven).

God created all things by His Word. "The worlds were framed by the Word of God." (Hebrews 11:3).

2. THEORY OF EVOLUTION.

Some men try to explain the world without God. They think that the material of which the universe is formed was always here, and that through very long periods of time it has changed or "evolved" to its present form. According to this view man is an accident of no great importance, being merely a highly developed form of animal life. But the Bible says, "In the beginning God" (Genesis 1:1). "All things were made by Him" (John 1:3).

3. BODY AND SOUL.

Man is a spirit dwelling in a body. The body in itself is a wonderful creation of God. It has many members, such as eyes and ears, which serve the soul. The eyes see, not for themselves but for the soul; the ears hear for the soul; the soul speaks through the mouth; the feet walk where the soul wants to go; the hands do what the soul directs.

The soul also has powers of its own, such as reason, memory, imagination, will, feelings. On his spiritual side man resembles God. The likeness man had to God at creation was a spiritual likeness. By falling into sin man has weakened the powers of his soul (lost the image of God). But still the soul is the important side of man. I *am* a soul. I *have* a body. The body cannot exist by itself. When the soul departs from it at the call of God, the body is dead.

SCRIPTURE READING
Genesis 1

FOR CLASS DISCUSSION

In the Notes there is a Scripture passage: "God breathed into man's nostrils the breath of life." Has God a body, lungs, and breath? What is God? If He put anything of Himself into man, what would it have to be?

If a man made a lawn-mower, and the lawn-mower tried to be a pencil sharpener, would it be very successful? Why not? If a typewriter wanted to make music like a piano, would it be successful? Why not? If man was made to love and serve God, how only can he be successful? If a man is rich, powerful, and famous, but does not believe in God, is he a successful man?

PRAYER

"O God, Thou hast made us for Thyself, and our hearts cannot rest until they rest in Thee." Let my heart rest in Thee, Father, and find joy in all Thy works. Amen.

LESSON 16

THE FIRST ARTICLE
GOD'S PROVIDENCE

109. Does God still care for His creatures?

Yes, I believe that He gives me *"food and raiment, home and family, and all my property; that He daily provides abundantly for all the needs of my life, protects me from all danger, and guards and keeps me from all evil."*

110. Do we not work for our food and other things we need?

Yes, but all our work would not keep us alive if God did not maintain His creation. (See NOTES, 1. Dependence on God.)

> The eyes of all wait upon Thee, and Thou givest them their meat in due season. Thou openest Thine hand and satisfiest the desire of every living thing. Ps. 145:15, 16.

111. What does this mean, "He protects me from all danger"?

It means that God watches over those who trust in Him, and keeps them safe.

> The angel of the Lord encampeth round about them that fear Him, and delivereth them. Ps. 34:7.

There shall no evil befall thee, neither shall any plague come nigh thy dwelling. For He shall give His angels charge over thee, to keep thee in all thy ways. They shall bear thee up in their hands, lest thou dash thy foot against a stone. Ps. 91:10, 12.

112.   May we foolishly run into danger and expect God to save us?

No, we are not to tempt God. (See Notes, 2. Tempting God.)

Thou shalt not tempt the Lord thy God. Matthew 4:7.

113.   How does God guard and keep us from all evil?

He is with us, and nothing can happen to us except what God permits. (See Notes, 3. Trusting God.)

Yea, though I walk through the valley of the shadow of death, I will fear no evil; for Thou art with me. Ps. 23:4.

Are not two sparrows sold for a farthing? And one of them shall not fall on the ground without your Father. But the very hairs of your head are all numbered. Fear ye not therefore; ye are of more value than many sparrows. Matthew 10:29, 31.

114.   But does not even the child of God sometimes meet misfortunes?

Yes, but God turns them to blessings. (See Notes, 4. Misfortunes Turned to Blessings.)

We know that all things work together for good to them that love God. Rom. 8:28.

Ye thought evil against me, but God meant it unto good. Gen. 50:20.

NOTES

1. DEPENDENCE ON GOD.

The world came into being because God willed it. It remains in existence only because God continues to will it. The earth revolves around the sun because God so wills, and without the warmth of the sun we could not live on the earth. The earth is surrounded with a blanket of air because God so wills, and without that air we could not live on the earth. Plants grow from seeds and produce more seeds because from creation God has willed that each plant should bring forth seed after its kind, and without the harvest of seeds we could not live. We could not make one seed that would grow. We are dependent on God. Life is possible only because God maintains His creation. "In Him we live and move and have our being." (Acts 17:28).

2. TEMPTING GOD.

Jesus refused to leap from the roof of the temple when the devil tempted Him to do so. God indeed has promised to protect us from danger, but He expects us to use the good sense He gave us, and not run into danger needlessly. To leap from a roof and expect God to catch you is tempting (trying) God. To neglect the laws of health and then say that God has sent you sickness is to blame God for something for which you should blame yourself.

3. TRUSTING GOD.

This is God's world and we are God's children. As a child feels safe in its father's house, so we may feel safe in our Father's world. There are evil men in the world who do not obey God's laws, and there are evil angels who are God's enemies; but we do not need to be afraid. "I will say of the Lord, He is my refuge and my fortress; my God, in Him will I trust" (Psalm 91:2). See question 24, lesson 3. As Luther said:

> Though devils all the world should fill,
> All watching to devour us,
> We tremble not, we fear no ill,
> They cannot overpow'r us.

4. MISFORTUNES TURNED TO BLESSINGS.

God does not promise that His children shall never meet sorrow or suffering in this world. We, too, are poor sinners, and therefore subject to the sorrow that came into the world with sin. But God turns even our sorrows into blessings. They teach us patience and faith, gentleness and courage. Not even death is an evil to the children of God. God turns it into a door by which we enter into everlasting life.

SCRIPTURE READING

II Kings 6:8-17

FOR CLASS DISCUSSION

Would you go into a house where there was smallpox or scarlet fever? Why not? If you felt that God wanted you to go into that house (perhaps as a nurse), would you be afraid to go? If a physician were called to the house, would he go? If they sent for a minister, would he go? What is the difference between someone going who has no business there, and the calls made by nurse or doctor or pastor?

Jesus fed a great crowd of people with a few loaves of bread, and another time He turned water into wine.

Who turns the water in the ground into grape juice in the grape? Who turns the bushel of wheat that is sown in the ground into ten or twenty bushels that are harvested? What is the difference between the miracles that Jesus did, and the everyday miracles in the vine and the wheat plant?

PRAYER

Bless the Lord, O my soul; and all that is within me, bless His holy name. Bless the Lord, O my soul, and forget not all His benefits; who forgiveth all thine iniquities; who healeth all thy diseases; who redeemeth thy life from destruction; who crowneth thee with loving kindness and tender mercies. Amen.

LESSON 17

THE FIRST ARTICLE

GOD'S LOVE AND OUR DUTY

115. What moves God to care for us?

He does this purely out of fatherly and divine goodness and mercy, without any merit or worthiness in me. (See NOTES, 1. God's Goodness.)

> It is of the Lord's mercies that we are not consumed, because His compassions fail not. Lam. 3:22.
>
> Like as a father pitieth his children, so the Lord pitieth them that fear Him. Ps. 103:13.

116. Are we worthy of this goodness?

No, He does it without any merit or worthiness in us.

> I am not worthy of the least of all the mercies and of all the truth which Thou hast showed unto Thy servant. Gen. 32:10.

117. Since God is so good to us, what is our duty?

For all which I am in duty bound to thank, praise, serve, and obey Him. (See NOTES, 2. Serving God.)

> O give thanks unto the Lord, for He is good; for His mercy endureth forever. Ps. 107:1.
>
> Let everything that hath breath praise the Lord. Praise ye the Lord. Ps. 150:6.
>
> Serve the Lord with gladness. Ps. 100:2.
>
> Obey my voice and I will be your God. Jer. 7:23.

118. What do we mean when we say at the end of the explanation of the First Article, "This is most certainly true"?

We thereby express our firm belief that God has created us and still cares for us.

> I will sing of the mercies of the Lord forever; with my mouth will I make known Thy faithfulness to all generations. Ps. 89:1.

NOTES

1. GOD'S GOODNESS.

God has created a wonderful world for us to live in. Beneath the surface of the earth are coal and oil, so useful to us, and the various metals like iron and copper and aluminum. On the surface of the earth plants grow and provide us with food. To make plant life possible, a wonderful watering system is in operation. The sun draws water from the sea into the air, the clouds carry the water over the land, and there it falls as rain.

To usefulness God has added beauty. Mountains and lakes, fields and streams, trees and flowers, all gladden the heart of man. There is color for man's eye to see, and music for his ear to hear. God is good.

All this God has provided and continues to maintain for man, who is not worthy; who has sinned and rebelled against God and despised His law. But God "maketh His sun to rise on the evil and on the good, and sendeth rain on the just and on the unjust." Matthew 5:45.

2. SERVING GOD.

Since God is so good to us, we should be grateful to Him. There is no better way to thank and praise Him than to use in His service the gifts He bestows upon us.

Our eyes should read His Word, our ears hear it, our minds remember and meditate on it.

Our tongues should sing His praise and proclaim His truth.

Our hands and feet should be swift and active in errands of mercy to our fellow men, that they may see our good works and glorify our Father in heaven.

Our possessions are God's gifts to us. We should remember that it is God's wealth, and use it in a way pleasing to Him.

Our talents will bring us the most enjoyment if those talents are dedicated to the service of God.

Bless the Lord, O my soul; and all that is within me, bless His holy name (Psalm 103:1).

SCRIPTURE READING
Psalm 121

FOR CLASS DISCUSSION

If you could go to any store in town and buy anything you wanted, what would you buy? Now see how many things you can list, which you have from God, and which are not for sale in any store.

If a man received a pension from the government, and gambled away his pension money, what would you think of him? Does everyone use wisely the gifts we have from God? Would God have a right to withhold those gifts? Does He do so? What does that prove in regard to God?

PRAYER

I thank Thee, dear heavenly Father, for Thy goodness to me and to all mankind. Help me to show my gratitude by the way I use Thy gifts. Amen.

LESSON 18

THE SECOND ARTICLE, OF REDEMPTION

119. Which is the Second Article of the Creed?

*And in Jesus Christ His only Son, our Lord;
who was conceived by the Holy Ghost,
born of the Virgin Mary; suffered under
Pontius Pilate, was crucified, dead, and
buried; He descended into hell; the third
day He rose again from the dead; He
ascended into heaven, and sitteth on the
right hand of God the Father Almighty;
from thence He shall come to judge the
quick and the dead.*

120. What does this mean?

*I believe that Jesus Christ, true God, begotten
of the Father from eternity, and also true
man, born of the Virgin Mary, is my
Lord; who has redeemed me, a lost and
condemned creature, bought me and
freed me from all sins, from death, and
from the power of the devil; not with
silver and gold, but with His holy and
precious blood, and with His innocent
sufferings and death; in order that I
might be His own, live under Him in His*

kingdom, and serve Him in everlasting righteousness, innocence and blessedness; even as He is risen from the dead, and lives and reigns to all eternity. This is most certainly true.

121.   Of whom does the Second Article treat?

Of Jesus Christ, the Son of God, my Redeemer. (See NOTES, 1. Jesus, and 2. Christ.)

122.   Whom did Christ redeem?

He redeemed me and all men. (See NOTES, 3. Redemption.)

> There is one God and one Mediator between God and men, the man Christ Jesus, who gave Himself a ransom for all. I Tim. 2:5, 6.

123.   Why was it necessary for Christ to redeem men?

Because we are all lost sinners by nature, condemned by God's holy law.

> There is no difference, for all have sinned and come short of the glory of God; being justified freely by His grace, through the redemption that is in Christ Jesus. Rom. 3:22-24.

NOTES

1.   JESUS.

The name Jesus was given to the Son of Mary by God through His holy angel. Jesus is the same name as Joshua In Hebrews 4:8 Jesus is used for Joshua. The name means, "the Lord saves." Thou shalt call His name Jesus; for He shall save His people from their sins. Matthew 1:21.

2. CHRIST.

In Old Testament times the prophets of God often spoke of the great Prophet who was coming. (See Deuteronomy 18:18.) Sometimes they spoke of the great kingdom which this Prophet would establish. (See Isaiah 9:6, 7.) Sometimes they spoke of this Prophet offering a sacrifice to God for the sins of His people, as the high priest did in the temple. (See Isaiah 53:4, 6 and verse 10.)

Since high priests and kings were anointed with oil as a sign of their office (See Leviticus 8:12; I Samuel 16:13), the people came to think of this great coming Prophet as "the Anointed One." In their language that was "the Messiah." (See John 4:25, 26.) We still sometimes call Jesus the Messiah. Occasionally you hear of a church called Messiah Lutheran Church. Old Testament prophecies which speak of Jesus and His work are called Messianic prophecies.

When the New Testament was written, Greek was the most common language of that part of the world where the writers lived. The word Messiah translated into Greek became "Christos," which also means "the Anointed One." From that we have the name "Christ."

3. REDEMPTION.

To redeem means to buy back. If you borrowed money, you might give a pledge to make the lender sure you would repay him. The pledge might be your watch, or a note, or a mortgage on your house. When you paid the debt you would "redeem" — buy back — your watch, or note, or mortgage. Sometimes in slavery days a slave would be redeemed. Someone would pay his owner the value of the slave in order to free him, and the slave would be a free man.

Jesus Christ bought us back out of slavery to sin, and made us God's free children. (See John 8:34 and 36). So Jesus Christ is our Redeemer.

SCRIPTURE READING

Matthew 1:18-25

FOR CLASS DISCUSSION

If a man mortgaged his home for one thousand dollars, how could he buy back (redeem) his home? If he pledged his watch for a small debt of five dollars, how could he redeem his watch? Would he be willing to give as much to redeem his watch as to redeem his home? What determines the amount a man would be willing to pay to redeem a pledged article? Could our souls be redeemed from sin by the payment of money? See Psalm 49:6-8 and Matthew 16:26. What price did Christ pay for the redemption of our souls? What does that show regarding the value God places on our souls?

PRAYER

Lord Jesus Christ, I thank Thee that Thou hast redeemed me, a lost sinner, and made me free from sin and death. Help me to live under Thee in Thy kingdom as a child of God. Amen.

THE SECOND ARTICLE

THE PERSON OF CHRIST

124. What does the explanation of the Second Article say of the Person of the Redeemer?

I believe that Jesus Christ, true God, begotten of the Father from eternity, and also true man, born of the Virgin Mary, is my Lord.

125. Why do you believe that Jesus Christ is true God?

Because the Bible calls Him God, shows that He has the attributes of God, does works which only God can do, and receives the honor which belongs to God alone. (See NOTES, 1. Jesus Christ Is God.)

> Thou art the Christ, the Son of the living God. Matthew 16:16.
>
> All power is given unto me in heaven and in earth . . . . and lo, I am with you alway. Matthew 28:18, 20.
>
> Thy sins be forgiven thee. Matthew 9:2.
>
> At the name of Jesus every knee should bow. Phil. 2:10.

126. Why do you believe that Jesus Christ is true man?

Because the Bible shows that He was born, grew, suffered and died as a man. (See NOTES, 2. Jesus Christ Is Man.)

JESUS CRUCIFIED

Unto you is born this day in the city of David
a Savior, which is Christ the Lord. Luke 2:11.

Jesus increased in wisdom and stature. Luke
2:52.

I thirst. John 19:28.

Christ died for our sins according to the
Scriptures. I Cor. 15:3.

127. Why was it necessary for Christ to be both God
and man?

True man He must be that He might put
Himself under the law, suffer and die
for our sins; true God He must be that
He might thus merit for all men forgiveness of sin and life eternal.

When the fulness of the time was come, God
sent forth His Son, born of a woman, born
under the law, to redeem them that were under
the law. Gal. 4:4, 5.

Forasmuch then as the children are partakers
of flesh and blood, He also Himself likewise
took part of the same; that through death He
might destroy him that had the power of death,
that is, the devil, and deliver them who through
fear of death were all their lifetime subject to
bondage. Heb. 2:14, 15.

128. What words of the Creed itself describe the Person
of the Redeemer?

And (I believe) in Jesus Christ His only Son,
our Lord; who was conceived by the
Holy Ghost, born of the Virgin Mary.
(See Notes, 3. Jesus Christ, the God-
Man, Is My Lord.)

NOTES

1. JESUS CHRIST IS GOD.

He was called God by His disciples and accepted the name. "Thou art the Christ, the Son of the living God." Matthew 16:16.

Jesus claimed God as His Father. "It is my Father that honoreth me, of whom ye say that He is your God." John 8:54.

God claimed Jesus as His Son. "This is my beloved Son, in whom I am well pleased; hear ye Him." Matthew 17:5.

Jesus said that He is eternal, John 8:58; all powerful, Matthew 28:18; everywhere present, Matthew 28:20. "All power is given unto me in heaven and in earth." Matthew 28:18.

Jesus said that He came down from heaven. "And now, O Father, glorify Thou me with Thine own self with the glory which I had with Thee before the world was." John 17:5.

He did miracles which no man can do. "No man can do these miracles that Thou doest, except God be with him." John 3:2.

He rose from the dead on the third day. "Ye seek Jesus of Nazareth, which was crucified: He is risen; He is not here." Mark 16:6.

He ascended into heaven. "This same Jesus, which is taken up from you into heaven, shall so come in like manner as ye have seen Him go into heaven." Acts 1:11.

2. JESUS CHRIST IS MAN.

He was born of a woman.   Luke 2:11; Galatians 4:4.
He grew as human children grow.   Luke 2:52.
He ate and drank to sustain life; He knew hunger and thirst.   Matthew 4:2; John 4:7.

He knew joy and sorrow. Luke 10:21; John 11:35.
He needed sleep and rest. Mark 4:38; Mark 6:31;
John 4:6.
He needed to pray. Mark 1:35; Luke 11:1.
He could suffer and die. Matthew 16:21.

3. JESUS CHRIST, THE GOD-MAN, IS MY LORD.

Ye call me Master and Lord, and ye say well, for so
I am. John 13:13.

One is your Master, even Christ. Matthew 23:10.

Then shall the King say unto them on His right hand,
Come, ye blessed of my Father, inherit the kingdom prepared for you from the foundation of the world. Matthew
25:34.

What think ye of Christ? Whose son is He? They
say unto Him, The son of David. He saith unto them,
How then doth David in Spirit call Him Lord? Matthew
22:42, 43.

The Lord hath need of them. Matthew 21:3.

The Son of man is Lord even of the sabbath day.
Matthew 12:8.

Not every one that saith unto me, Lord, Lord, shall
enter into the kingdom of heaven; but he that doeth the
will of my Father which is in heaven. Matthew 7:21.

SCRIPTURE READING
Isaiah 53

FOR CLASS DISCUSSION

Complete this passage, which we had in a previous
lesson: "The wages of sin is ...." We said
God is holy, righteous, merciful and truthful. Which
of these attributes requires the punishment of sin? Could
not God just forget about sin and forgive everyone? Does

the government forget about murders, kidnapping, counterfeiting? What would happen to the government that failed to enforce its laws?

God must punish sin. How can He punish sin and forgive the sinners? Could one of us take the punishment for the world's sin? Give reasons for your answer. If we are not to bear the punishment for our sins, who else is there to bear it? Animals? Men? Angels? God?

PRAYER

We thank Thee, dear Lord Jesus, that Thou didst come into the world to suffer and die for our sins. Help us to repent of them truly and to ask forgiveness in Thy name. Amen.

LESSON 20

THE SECOND ARTICLE
THE WORK OF CHRIST

129. What does the explanation of the Second Article say of the work of the Redeemer?

Who has redeemed me, a lost and condemned creature, bought me and freed me from all sins, from death, and from the power of the devil; not with silver and gold, but with His holy and precious blood, and with His innocent sufferings and death.

130. Where and how did this take place?

He *"suffered under Pontius Pilate, was crucified, dead, and buried."* (See NOTES, 1. Passion History.)

131. How do you know this was for you?

The prophets foretold that Christ would suffer for others, Christ Himself said that He gave His life for us, and His apostles were told to proclaim this Gospel to all the world. (See NOTES, 2. Atonement.)

All we like sheep have gone astray; we have turned every one to his own way, and the Lord hath laid on Him the iniquity of us all. Isa. 53:6.

I am the Good Shepherd; the Good Shepherd
giveth His life for the sheep. John 10:11.

Go ye into all the world, and preach the
Gospel to every creature. He that believeth and
is baptized shall be saved. Mark 16:15, 16.

God . . . hath made Him to be sin for us who
knew no sin, that we might be made the
righteousness of God in Him. II Cor. 5:21.

132. From what did Christ thus redeem you?

He redeemed me from all sins, from death,
and from the power of the devil.

Who shall lay anything to the charge of God's
elect? It is God that justifieth. Who is he that
condemneth? It is Christ that died, yea rather,
that is risen again, who is even at the right
hand of God, who also maketh intercession for
us. Rom. 8:33, 34. (Redeemed from the curse
of sin.)

O death, where is thy sting? O grave, where
is thy victory? The sting of death is sin, and
the strength of sin is the law. But thanks be to
God, which giveth us the victory through our
Lord Jesus Christ. I Cor. 15:55-57. (Redeemed
from the fear of death.)

Heb. 2:14, 15. See Question 127. (Redeemed
from the power of the devil.)

133. What price did Christ pay for your redemption?

He redeemed me not with silver and gold,
but with His holy and precious blood,
and with His innocent sufferings and
death. (See Notes, 3. Lamb of God.)

Ye know that ye were not redeemed with cor-
ruptible things as silver and gold, ... but
with the precious blood of Christ, as of a lamb
without blemish and without spot. I Pet. 1:18,
19.

NOTES

1. THE PASSION HISTORY.

The four Gospels, Matthew, Mark, Luke and John, tell us of the suffering and death of Jesus Christ. Each writer gives some details that the others omit, so to get the complete story it is necessary to put the four accounts together. This has been done by men who have studied the Gospels carefully, and we have the result in our Hymnal. There the Passion History (Passion means Suffering) is divided into seven parts, as follows:

    I. Jesus' Readiness to Suffer and Die.
    II. Jesus' Agony of Soul in Gethsemane.
    III. Jesus Before the Sanhedrin.
    IV. Jesus Before Pilate.
    V. Jesus Condemned to Death.
    VI. Jesus' Death on the Cross.
    VII. Jesus' Burial.

2. ATONEMENT.

To atone is to make up for something wrong. If you have been rude to a person, you show that person special kindness to atone for your rudeness.

Jesus' suffering and death for our sins is called the Atonement. He atoned for our sins; He did something to make up (to God) for our wrongdoing. Because we are thus redeemed and brought back to God as His children, it has been pointed out that the word can be spelled At-one-ment. The Atonement makes it possible for us to be "at one" with God.

Jesus' suffering and death is called a "vicarious" Atonement. A vicar is one who acts for someone else, in someone else's stead. Jesus suffered in our stead. He bore the lightning of God's wrath that we might enjoy the sunshine of God's love.

3. LAMB OF GOD.

In the Old Testament temple, lambs were offered as sacrifices for sin. Since Jesus is the perfect sacrifice for sin, He is called the Lamb of God. See how this idea is expressed in the following places:

Isaiah 53:6, 7; John 1:29; I Peter 1:19; Revelation 7:14.

The Gloria in Excelsis (Glory to God in the highest).

The Agnus Dei (Lamb of God), Communion Service.

SCRIPTURE READING

John 19

FOR CLASS DISCUSSION

If a boy had broken a costly store window while playing, would he like to see the police car stop at his house? How would he feel? But suppose he had told his father all about it, and his father had agreed to pay the boy's debt. Would that change the boy's feeling? In what way?

Have we broken God's law? How many of us? What does the law demand of the law-breaker? But if some one else has already paid the penalty for us, what effect does that have on us? Death is the messenger of the Law, sent to bring us before the Judge. But suppose, when we stand before the Judge, we discover that He is the very one who loved us enough to pay the penalty for us. How would we feel then? Now do you understand Romans 8:33, 34?

PRAYER

Father, I have sinned against Thee, and have deserved everlasting punishment. But Jesus, my Redeemer, has suffered in my stead, and I claim the forgiveness which Thou hast promised in His name. The blood of Jesus Christ, Thy Son, cleanses me from all sin. Amen.

LESSON 21

THE SECOND ARTICLE
THE PURPOSE OF REDEMPTION

134. What does the explanation of the Second Article say of the purpose of Christ's redeeming you?

He redeemed me *"in order that I might be His own, live under Him in His kingdom, and serve Him in everlasting righteousness, innocence, and blessedness; even as He is risen from the dead, and lives and reigns to all eternity. This is most certainly true."*

135. How does the Creed describe the glory that followed Christ's suffering?

He descended into hell; the third day He rose again from the dead; He ascended into heaven, and sitteth on the right hand of God the Father Almighty; from thence He shall come to judge the quick and the dead. (See NOTES, 1. Christ's Descent into Hell; 2. Christ's Resurrection; 3. Christ's Ascension into Heaven.)

136. What does this mean?

It means that God has triumphed over wickedness and sin, and will triumph forever.

137. What benefit is that to you?

> By faith I am God's child and live under
> Christ in His kingdom. (See NOTES, 4.
> Christ's Kingdom.)

>> He that believeth and is baptized shall be
>> saved. Mark 16:16.

138. For what purpose will Christ come again?

> He will come to judge the quick (living)
> and the dead. (See NOTES, 5. Judgment
> Day.)

>> We must all appear before the judgment seat
>> of Christ; that every one may receive the things
>> done in his body, according to that he hath
>> done, whether it be good or bad. II Cor. 5:10.

139. What will then be the benefit of Christ's having
redeemed you?

> I shall serve Him in everlasting righteousness,
> innocence and blessedness.

>> In my Father's house are many mansions; if
>> it were not so I would have told you. I go to
>> prepare a place for you. And if I go and pre-
>> pare a place for you, I will come again and
>> receive you unto myself; that where I am, there
>> ye may be also. John 14:2, 3.

140. What do we mean when we end the explanation of
the Second Article with the words, "This is most
certainly true"?

> We thereby express our firm belief that Jesus
> Christ, God's Son, died for our sins, and
> thus redeemed us for a blessed life with
> Him here in time and hereafter in eter-
> nity.

NOTES

1. CHRIST'S DESCENT INTO HELL.

Of Christ's descent into hell we know little. It cannot have been for the purpose of suffering, for on the cross He said, "It is finished." The only passage in the Bible which speaks of the descent into hell, I Peter 3:19, indicates that it was for the purpose of triumphing over God's enemies.

2. CHRIST'S RESURRECTION.

On the third day He rose again from the dead. He had said, "I lay down my life that I might take it again. . . . I have power to lay it down, and I have power to take it again." John 10:17, 18. On Easter Sunday morning His friends found the grave open and empty. On the same day He appeared to them and said, "Behold my hands and my feet, that it is I myself; handle me and see, for a spirit hath not flesh and bones as you see me have." Luke 24:39.

3. CHRIST'S ASCENSION INTO HEAVEN.

For a period of forty days after His resurrection Jesus appeared to His disciples, not constantly, but from time to time. On the fortieth day He led them out of Jerusalem to the Mount of Olives, and there "while they beheld, He was taken up; and a cloud received Him out of their sight." Acts 1:9.

4. CHRIST'S KINGDOM.

That Jesus sits at God's right hand means that He has a position of honor and authority. "All power is given unto me in heaven and in earth," He says. Matthew 28:18. "He raised Him from the dead, and set Him at His own right hand in the heavenly place, far above all principality and power and might and dominion, and every name that is named, not only in this world but also in that which is to come, and hath put all things under His feet, and gave Him to be the head over all things to the Church." Ephesians 1:20-22.

Jesus now rules over all things. Even wicked men, who do not want Him for their King, are ruled by Him. This is called His **kingdom of power.**

In the Church He is King in a special sense, because the members of the Church are His own people who love Him and serve Him gladly. Here He rules by love, so the Church is called His **kingdom of grace.**

When He comes again to judge the world, He will take His redeemed to Himself in heaven to serve Him in everlasting blessedness. That will be His **kingdom of glory.**

5. JUDGMENT DAY.

We do not know when the Judgment Day will be. "Of that day and that hour knoweth no man." Mark 13:32. People who pretend to know exactly when it will be show that they do not know their Bible. We are to be ready for it at any time. "Watch therefore, for ye know neither the day nor the hour wherein the Son of man cometh." Matthew 25:13.

SCRIPTURE READING

Matthew 28

FOR CLASS DISCUSSION

How much power has God? If someone had more power, who would be God? If God is God, will His plans and His will fail? Can evil men and evil angels cause God's plans to fail? In a war between right and wrong which will win in the end? Which side would you want to be on?

Suppose a man were in debt, and someone else paid the debt for him. But when they came and told the man his debt was paid, he refused to believe it. What would you say of him? Jesus paid the debt of our sins. For how many people? Do all people receive the benefit of Jesus' redemption? Who does not?

PRAYER

Lord Jesus, I desire to live with Thee in Thy glory. To that end help me to live now in Thy grace, to cling to Thee and Thy promises by faith, and to love Thee even as Thou hast loved me. Amen.

Peter's Pentecost Sermon

LESSON 22

THE THIRD ARTICLE, OF SANCTIFICATION

141. Which is the Third Article of the Creed?

> *I believe in the Holy Ghost; the Holy Christian Church, the communion of saints; the forgiveness of sins; the resurrection of the body; and the life everlasting. Amen.*

142. What does this mean?

> *I believe that I cannot by my own reason or strength believe in Jesus Christ, my Lord, or come to Him; but the Holy Ghost has called me through the Gospel, enlightened me with His gifts, and sanctified and preserved me in the true faith; in like manner as He calls, gathers, enlightens, and sanctifies the whole Christian Church on earth, and preserves it in union with Jesus Christ in the one true faith; in which Christian Church He daily forgives abundantly all my sins, and the sins of all believers, and at the last day will raise up me and all the dead,*

*and will grant everlasting life to me and
to all who believe in Christ. This is most
certainly true.*

143. Of whom does the Third Article treat?

Of God the Holy Ghost who sanctifies me.
(See NOTES, 1. Sanctification.)

> But ye are washed, but ye are sanctified, but
> ye are justified in the name of the Lord Jesus,
> and by the Spirit of our God. I Cor. 6:11.

144. Who is the Holy Ghost?

He is the third person of the Trinity, one
with the Father and the Son. (See
NOTE 2, Lesson 14.)

145. Why do you believe that the Holy Ghost is true
God?

Because the Bible calls Him God, shows that
He has the attributes of God, does works
which only God can do, and receives
the honor which belongs to God alone.
(See NOTES, 2. The Third Person of the
Trinity.)

> Know ye not that ye are the temple of God,
> and that the Spirit of God dwelleth in you?
> I Cor. 3:16.
> God hath revealed them unto us by His
> Spirit; for the Spirit searcheth all things, yea,
> the deep things of God. I Cor. 2:10.
> Except a man be born of water and of the
> Spirit, he cannot enter into the kingdom of God.
> John 3:5.
> Go ye therefore and teach all nations, baptiz-
> ing them in the name of the Father and of the
> Son and of the Holy Ghost. Matthew 28:19.

1. Sanctification.   **NOTES**

In the communion service there is a chant called "The Sanctus." "Sanctus" is Latin for "holy." The chant is called The Sanctus because it begins with the words, "Holy, holy, holy."

To sanctify means to make holy. In the broad sense all that the Holy Spirit does for us is a work of sanctification. He calls us by the Gospel, that is, He brings us to faith in Christ and makes us members of the communion of saints (holy persons) whose sins are forgiven. He enlightens us with His gifts, that is, He gives us more and more understanding of how we ought to live as God's children. He sanctifies us (in the narrow sense), that is, He gives us pleasure in good works and power to do them. (See Question 150.)

2. The Third Person of the Trinity.

There are five Scripture passages in this lesson. In the last one the third person of the Trinity is called the Holy Ghost. In the other four He is called the Spirit of God, or simply the Spirit. Ghost and Spirit mean the same.

Other names for the Holy Spirit are: The Comforter (John 14:16, John 14:26, John 15:26, John 16:7) ; the Spirit of Truth (John 14:17, John 15:26, John 16:13) ; the Spirit of Christ (Romans 8:9) ; the Spirit of life (Romans 8:2) ; the eternal Spirit (Hebrews 9:14).

SCRIPTURE READING
Acts 2:1-13

FOR CLASS DISCUSSION
Is the Holy Spirit a thing?
a force?
an influence?
a person?

Give reasons for your answer. What is said of the Holy Spirit in I Corinthians 2:11? In I Corinthians 12:11? In Ephesians 4:30? Are these personal or impersonal qualities?

Why is He called the "Holy" Spirit? Does a Christian have the Holy Spirit or does the Holy Spirit have the Christian?

PRAYER

Come, Holy Spirit, come;
Let Thy bright beams arise;
Dispel the sorrow from our minds,
The darkness from our eyes. Amen.

LESSON 23

THE THIRD ARTICLE
THE WORK OF THE HOLY SPIRIT

146. What does the Holy Spirit do for you?

He brings me to Christ, that is, He *calls me by the Gospel, enlightens me with His gifts, sanctifies, and keeps me in the true faith.* (See NOTES, 1. Conversion.)

> No man can say that Jesus is the Lord but by the Holy Ghost. I Cor. 12:3.

147. Why must the Holy Spirit do this for you?

Because I cannot by my own reason or strength believe in Jesus Christ, my Lord, or come to Him.

> The natural man receiveth not the things of the Spirit of God. I Cor. 2:14.

148. How has the Holy Spirit called you by the Gospel?

He has caused the Gospel of Jesus Christ to be written in the Bible, and through that Gospel He has worked faith in my heart.

> Faith cometh by hearing, and hearing by the Word of God. Rom. 10:17.

149. How does the Holy Spirit enlighten you with His gifts?

He gives me the light of the true knowledge of God, and of God's salvation in Jesus Christ. (See NOTES, 2. Gifts of the Spirit.)

(115)

> God, who commanded the light to shine out of darkness, hath shined in our hearts to give the light of the knowledge of the glory of God in the face of Jesus Christ. II Cor. 4:6.

150. How does the Holy Spirit sanctify you?

He gives me pleasure in good works and power to do them. (See NOTES, 3. Good Works.)

> It is God which worketh in you both to will and to do of His good pleasure. Phil. 2:13.

151. How does the Holy Spirit keep you in the true faith?

He leads me to use the Word of God faithfully, to watch and pray diligently, to hate and forsake sin, and to go to the Lord's Supper regularly.

152. What is the means through which the Holy Spirit works?

He works through the Word of God. (See NOTES, 3. Means of Grace.)

> Sanctify them through Thy truth; Thy Word is truth. John 17:17.

NOTES

1. CONVERSION.

Conversion means "turning." We are by nature turned away from God and turned toward sin. When the Holy Spirit turns us away from sin and toward God, He converts us. "Turn Thou me, and I shall be turned; for Thou art the Lord my God. Surely after that I was turned, I repented" (Jer. 31:18, 19).

Repentance is what takes place in us when we are converted. It means "a change of heart." Repentance includes two things: a heart-felt sorrow for our sins, and a heart-felt trust in God as the Forgiver of our sins.

2. Gifts of the Spirit.

First, the Word of God. "When He, the Spirit of truth, is come, He will guide you into all truth" (John 16:13). "Holy men of God spake as they were moved by the Holy Ghost." (II Peter 1:21).

Second, faith in Christ through hearing the Word. "Faith cometh by hearing, and hearing by the Word of God." (Romans 10:17).

Third, gifts useful in preaching and explaining the Word: knowledge and wisdom, I Corinthians 12:8; the ability to speak with other tongues, Acts 2:4, I Corinthians 14.

Fourth, signs to prove that the message is really from God: gifts of healing, the working of miracles, I Corinthians 12:9, 10.

Fifth, gifts that enable us to live according to the Word of God: love, I Corinthians 13; joy, peace, long-suffering, gentleness, goodness, faith, meekness, temperance, Galatians 5:22, 23.

Some of these gifts all Christians have, namely the Word, and faith, and a degree of ability to understand the Word and live according to it. Not all Christians have the same degree of ability. We are to grow in grace, II Peter 3:18.

Other gifts, like the gift of tongues, healing, and the working of other miracles, are not given to all Christians, but are given when and where the Holy Spirit wills. "All these worketh that one and the selfsame Spirit, dividing to every man severally, *as He will*." I Corinthians 12:11.

3. GOOD WORKS.

Good works are works that are pleasing to God; all
that a Christian thinks, speaks and does from faith, according to God's command, and to His honor and glory.

They are not good works unless done by Christians,
who are God's children by faith. "Without faith it is
impossible to please God" (Hebrews 11:6). If a child of
God gives to the poor because he knows God wants him
to love his neighbor as himself, and he wishes to do God's
will, it is a good work. If an unbeliever also gives to the
poor, perhaps for business reasons, it is not a good work
in the sight of God. "Though I bestow all my goods to
feed the poor . . . and have not love" (the proper motive,
which is a gift of the Spirit), "it profiteth me nothing"
(I Corinthians 13:3).

Good works do not save us. We cannot do good works
unless we are already saved, that is, God's children by
faith. God saves us by grace (unmerited kindness) for
Jesus' sake. "By grace are ye saved through faith, and
that not of yourselves. It is the gift of God, not of works,
lest any man should boast" (Ephesians 2:8, 9). But being
God's children by faith, we will do good works because it
is our nature to do them. "Faith, if it hath not works, is
dead, being alone" (James 2:17).

4. MEANS OF GRACE.

The means through which the Holy Spirit works and
strengthens faith in us are called the means of grace. They
are the Word of God and the Sacraments (Holy Baptism
and the Lord's Supper). Even in the Sacraments it is
the Word of God that "does such great things."

SCRIPTURE READING
I Corinthians 13

FOR CLASS DISCUSSION

Would it be proper to wish to have the gifts of the Spirit? Read Acts 8:18-20 and I Corinthians 12:31. How would one go about getting the gifts of the Spirit? Can we say to the Spirit of God, "Now I am ready; come and work on me"? What are the last three words of I Corinthians 12:11? What did Jesus say of the coming and going of the wind? John 3:8. Could a man in a sailboat command the wind to come and blow the boat where he wanted to go? But if he knew that in a certain latitude the wind always blows in a certain direction, what could he do? Could a rich man say to his servant, "Go out and get some of that sunshine and bring it in here"? But what could he do? Where can we find the Spirit of God at work? Read also Luke 11:13.

PRAYER

Holy Spirit, I thank Thee that Thou hast brought me to Christ, and pray that Thou wouldst enlighten, sanctify and keep me in that faith unto everlasting life. Amen.

LESSON 24

THE THIRD ARTICLE

THE HOLY CHRISTIAN CHURCH

153. Into what does the Holy Spirit call and gather us?

Into the Holy Christian Church. (See NOTES, 1. The Church.)

154. What is the Holy Christian Church?

It is the communion of saints, that is, all those who truly believe in Christ. (See NOTES, 2. Communion of Saints.)

> There is one body, and one Spirit, even as ye are called in one hope of your calling; one Lord, one faith, one baptism, one God and Father of all, who is above all, and through all, and in you all. Eph. 4:4-6.

155. Where is the Church found on earth?

Where the Word of God is taught in its truth and purity, and the Sacraments are administered according to Christ's institution.

> If ye continue in my Word, then are ye my disciples indeed. John 8:31.

156. Why are we in the Lutheran Church?

Because we believe that the Lutheran Church teaches the Word of God in truth and purity. (See NOTES, 3. The Lutheran Church.)

(120)

157. Does it make any difference to which denomination
one belongs?

Yes, the Word of God earnestly warns
against all false teaching and teachers.

> Beloved, believe not every spirit, but try the
> spirits whether they are of God; because many
> false prophets are gone out into the world.
> I John 4:1.
> If any man preach any other gospel unto you
> than that ye have received, let him be accursed.
> Gal. 1:9.

158. What is the Lord's commission to the Church?

Go ye therefore and teach all nations, baptizing them in the name of the Father,
and of the Son, and of the Holy Ghost;
teaching them to observe all things,
whatsoever I have commanded you.
Matthew 28:19, 20.

159. What is the duty of every Christian?

It is the Christian's duty to unite with a faithful congregation, and do his part in all
its work.

NOTES

1. THE CHURCH.

The word "church" comes from a Greek word that
means "belonging to the Lord." The Church is called
Christian because its members are believers in Christ. Acts
11:26. It is the Holy Christian Church because the sins
of its members are forgiven and they are God's children.
Sometimes it is called the Holy Catholic Church (not Roman Catholic); the word "catholic" meaning "universal"
or "for all."

2. THE COMMUNION OF SAINTS.

"Communion," as used here, means a body of people who have something in common. (Compare community, commonwealth.) What we have in common in the Church is our God, our Savior, our faith, our worship (See Ephesians 4:4-6, Question 154). We are a communion of "saints" because our sins are forgiven. "Saint" comes from the same root as "sanctify" (See NOTE 1, Lesson 22).

3. THE LUTHERAN CHURCH.

The Lutherans separated from the Roman Catholic Church in 1530, when the Augsburg Confession was adopted by the followers of Luther. This Confession is a statement of faith and is named for Augsburg, the city in Germany where it was first presented to the world. It also contains a list of things we do *not* believe — errors and abuses which had crept into the Church's doctrine and practice in the course of time. If the Roman Catholic Church had been willing to renounce the errors and return to the teaching of the apostles, the Lutherans would never have become a separate body. But since the Roman Church refused to correct the evils, the Lutherans separated themselves from it. Our Church is called the "Evangelical" Lutheran Church, which means that it preaches the Gospel. It is the largest of the Protestant denominations.

SCRIPTURE READING
Matthew 16:13-28

FOR CLASS DISCUSSION

Are not all churches alike? Do they not all have the same Lord? Are not Roman Catholics Christians? How do we know that one church is better than another? In Ephesians 4:5 how many faiths does St. Paul say the Christians have? But there are many differences today. How do we know what to believe? Where does the Christian faith come from? Which would be the best church, then?

PRAYER

Preserve Thy Church, O God, from error and unfaithfulness, and give her courage to proclaim the truth as it is in Christ Jesus unto the ends of the earth. Amen.

LESSON 25

THE THIRD ARTICLE
THE FORGIVENESS OF SINS

160. What is the third great truth we confess in this Article?

I believe in *"the forgiveness of sins."*

161. What does this mean?

I believe that in the Christian Church God *"daily forgives abundantly all my sins, and the sins of all believers."* (See NOTES, 1. Justification by Faith.)

> Let the wicked forsake his way, and the unrighteous man his thoughts; and let him return unto the Lord, and He will have mercy upon him, and to our God, for He will abundantly pardon. Isa. 55:7.
>
> Bless the Lord, O my soul, and forget not all His benefits; who forgiveth all thine iniquities. Ps. 103:2, 3.

162. Why do we need the forgiveness of sins daily and abundantly?

Because we daily sin much.

> There is no difference, for all have sinned and come short of the glory of God; being justified freely by His grace, through the redemption that is in Christ Jesus. Rom. 3:22-24.
>
> If we say that we have no sin, we deceive ourselves and the truth is not in us. If we confess our sins, He is faithful and just to forgive us our sins and to cleanse us from all unrighteousness. I John 1:8-9.

(124)

163.   How is it possible for God to forgive our sins?

Because Christ died for us (See Lesson 20).

> All we like sheep have gone astray ... and the Lord hath laid on Him the iniquity of us all. Isa. 53:6.
>
> (He) bare our sins in His own body on the tree. I Pet. 2:24.
>
> (God) hath made Him to be sin for us who knew no sin, that we might be made the righteousness of God in Him. II Cor. 5:21.

NOTES

1.   JUSTIFICATION BY FAITH.

A just person is one who is without sin in the sight of God.

We cannot justify ourselves.   No matter how many good deeds we do, they cannot hide the fact that we have also done evil, have sinned.   The Pharisee, in the story of the Pharisee and the publican, Luke 18:9-14, tried to justify himself, and was not justified.   To trust in one's works to make one righteous in God's sight is called work-righteousness.   It is a false hope.

"It is God that justifieth" (Romans 8:33).   Justification is the act of God in forgiving our sins. He pronounces us just, as a governor pardons a prisoner.   God does it for Christ's sake.   Because Christ suffered the punishment of our sins in our stead, we are forgiven.   We are pronounced not guilty.   "God was in Christ, reconciling the world unto Himself, *not imputing* their trespasses unto them" (II Corinthians 5:19).

God justifies *those who believe* that Christ died for them.   "That He (God) might be just, and the Justifier of him which believeth in Jesus . . . . Therefore we conclude that a man is *justified by faith,* without the deeds of the law" (Romans 3:26-28). This was one of the great principles of the Protestant Reformation.

Even our faith is a gift of God. "By grace are ye saved, through faith; and that not of yourselves. It is the gift of God, not of works, lest any man should boast." (Ephesians 2:8, 9). I believe that I cannot by my own reason or strength believe in Jesus Christ, my Lord, or come to Him; but the Holy Ghost has called me through the Gospel, etc.

SCRIPTURE READING

Psalm 103

FOR CLASS DISCUSSION

Does it make any difference if we sin? Will not God forgive our sins anyway? Whose sins does God forgive? How does one get to be a believer? What else does the Holy Spirit do for us besides calling and gathering us? Would the Holy Spirit do part of His work in us and not the rest? Then will believers want to sin, or want not to sin?

PRAYER

We thank Thee, Father, that Thou dost daily forgive our sins for Jesus' sake, and pray that through the grace of the Holy Spirit we may more and more hate and forsake sin. Amen.

LESSON 26

THE THIRD ARTICLE

RESURRECTION AND EVERLASTING LIFE

164. What is the final point of the faith we confess?

I believe in *"the resurrection of the body; and the life everlasting."*

165. What is the resurrection of the body?

At the last day all the dead will rise. Their bodies will be restored to life, and the souls reunited with their bodies. (See NOTES, 1. Resurrection.)

> The hour is coming in the which all that are in the graves shall hear His voice and shall come forth; they that have done good, unto the resurrection of life, and they that have done evil unto the resurrection of damnation. John 5:28, 29.
>
> Jesus said unto her, I am the resurrection and the life. He that believeth on me, though he were dead, yet shall he live. John 11:25.

166. What will follow the resurrection of the dead?

The judgment of all men.

> We must all appear before the judgment seat of Christ. II Cor. 5:10.

167. What will God give to His people in the judgment?

He will grant everlasting life to me and to all who believe in Christ.

> This is the will of Him that sent me, that everyone which seeth the Son and believeth on Him may have everlasting life. John 6:40.

168. What kind of a life will this be?

> It will be sinless, happy, and unending.

>> God shall wipe away all tears from their eyes; and there shall be no more death, neither sorrow nor crying. Rev. 21:4.

169. What will become of unbelievers?

> Because they have rejected God's grace, they shall exist in everlasting separation from God and from all good. (See NOTES, 2. Different States After Death.)

>> And these shall go away into everlasting punishment; but the righteous into life eternal. Matthew 25:46.

170. What do we mean when we end the Explanation of the Third Article with the words, "This is most certainly true"?

> We thereby express our firm belief that the Holy Spirit has called us into the Church and will keep us in grace unto everlasting life.

NOTES

1. RESURRECTION.

Before His death, Jesus said to His disciples, "In my Father's house are many mansions; if it were not so, I would have told you. I go to prepare a place for you. And if I go and prepare a place for you, I will come again and receive you unto myself, that where I am, there ye may be also" (John 14:2, 3). A few minutes later He said, "Because I live, ye shall live also" (John 14:19).

We know that Jesus rose from the dead on the third day, and that He had raised others from the dead. We also have His promise that He will raise us. The Christian therefore does not need to fear death; it is the door to a better life.

The New Testament is full of the doctrine of the resurrection. The longest passage on this subject is I Corinthians 15, called "the resurrection chapter." Read it.

2. DIFFERENT STATES AFTER DEATH.

At death each individual soul is judged and assigned to one of two places, heaven or hell. On the last day those souls will be reunited with their resurrected bodies, and the general judgment will take place.

The Roman Catholic Church teaches that there is a third place, called Purgatory, where souls that will finally reach heaven must first be "purged," that is, purified. According to this doctrine, the Church can help those souls out of Purgatory earlier by saying prayers and masses for them.

This doctrine is not found in God's Word. When Jesus told the story of the rich man and Lazarus, to show what happens after death, He named only two places, heaven and hell (Luke 16:19-31). To the penitent thief on the cross He said, "Today shalt thou be with me in paradise" (Luke 23:43). If there were a purgatory, that man who repented at the last minute after a life of sin would be one who must spend a long time in the place of purification. But Jesus said that on the same day of his death the man would be with Him in heaven.

Other doctrines which are taught as Christian, but are not, are that all men will be saved (Universalism), or that all will be given another chance to repent after death (Jehovah's Witnesses).

SCRIPTURE READING

Matthew 25:31-46

FOR CLASS DISCUSSION

Do you think we shall know and recognize each other in heaven? On what Scripture passage do you base your belief? Do you think that people who have died and gone to heaven know what takes place on earth? Can mediums and spiritualists bring them back to talk to the living? What do you think heaven will be like? What is the difference between everlasting life and eternal life?

PRAYER

O Lord Jesus Christ, when Thou shalt raise me up at the last day, let me stand before Thy judgment seat justified by faith, and enter into the joy of everlasting life. Amen.

PART III

THE LORD'S PRAYER

Lord, Teach Us to Pray

LESSON 27

PRAYER

171. What is prayer?

Prayer is a communion with God, in which we bring all our joys and sorrows to Him as our dear Friend. (See NOTES, 1. Prayer.)

172. Why do we pray?

Because God wants us to pray, and because we want to pray.

> And He spake a parable unto them to this end, that men ought always to pray. Luke 18:1. I will therefore that men pray everywhere. I Tim. 2:8.

173. Does God hear prayer?

Yes, we have His word that He does.

> It shall come to pass that before they call I will answer, and while they are yet speaking I will hear. Isa. 65:24.

174. Does God answer prayer?

He answers prayer according to His wisdom, which is much greater than ours.

175. What condition do we therefore add to many of our prayers?

If we are not sure what God's will is in the matter, we say, "If it be Thy will."

176. How must Christian prayer be offered?

In the name of Jesus, that is, in true faith.
(See NOTES, 2. Prayer in the Name of
Jesus.)

All things whatsoever ye shall ask in prayer,
believing, ye shall receive. Matthew 21:22.
Verily, verily, I say unto you, Whatsoever ye
shall ask the Father in my name, He will give
it you. John 16:23.

177. What prayer did Jesus teach us?

The Lord's Prayer.

178. What are the parts of the Lord's Prayer?

The Introduction.
The Seven Petitions.
The Conclusion.

NOTES

1. PRAYER.

Sometimes we think of prayer as consisting of petitions
only, that is, asking God for what we want. That is the
narrow sense of the word. Thus Luther, in explaining the
Second Commandment, says that we should call upon the
name of God in every time of need, and worship Him with
prayer, praise and thanksgiving.

But praising God and giving Him thanks are also
prayer. So for our definition of prayer we say it is a
communion with God in which we bring before Him all
our joys and sorrows. God is our dear Father through
Christ, and He is always in our minds. If anything pleasant, happy, joyful occurs, our first thought will be to tell
God about it and thank Him. If we have any need, sor-

row, fear, our first thought is to tell God about it and ask Him for His help.

Prayer is thus the very atmosphere in which the Christian lives. That is what the apostle means when he says, "Pray without ceasing" (I Thessalonians 5:17). The Christian enjoys constant communion with God. When you make use of that privilege to share with God everything that is in your heart, you are praying.

2. PRAYING IN JESUS' NAME.

The answer to Question 176 suggests that praying in Jesus' name and praying in faith are the same thing.

It is like this: suppose you went to a bank where you are not known and tried to draw out some money. The banker would say, "I do not know you; you have no money here." But suppose you went to that bank with a certified check signed by someone the banker knew. He would give you the money without question.

We have no merit of our own before God. As sinners we could not ask for blessings and expect to receive them. But Jesus died for our sins. If we believe that and accept Him as our Savior, then we have faith and are God's children. Then all the promises of God are ours in Christ. To be in faith is to be in Christ; to pray in faith is to pray not in our own name, but in His.

To many of our prayers we add the phrase, "In Jesus' name," or "This we ask for Jesus' sake." A prayer may be a Christian prayer, however, without having such a phrase in it; for example, the Lord's Prayer. Whenever we pray because we believe that Jesus died for us and that therefore God is our dear Father, we are praying in Jesus' name. Prayers that are not offered on the basis of Christ's merits are not Christian prayers and are not heard by God.

SCRIPTURE READING

Matthew 6:5-15

FOR CLASS DISCUSSION

Suppose you wanted to go on a picnic on a certain day, and prayed for fair weather. But when the day arrived, there had been so many sunny days that all the farmers were praying for rain for their crops. Could God answer your prayer and theirs? Which do you think it would be better for Him to answer? Would you want to make such decisions on the basis of your own wisdom? Then how should you have made your prayer in the first place?

If a little child asked for a burning candle to play with, would the child's father give it to him? What would the father likely do? Can you name something we may ask God for without adding, "if it be Thy will"?

PRAYER

Lord, teach us to pray. Let Thy Holy Spirit move us to bring all our joys and sorrows to Thee, rejoicing in this privilege of the children of God. Amen.

LESSON 28

THE INTRODUCTION

179. What is the Introduction to the Lord's Prayer?

Our Father, who art in heaven.

180. What does this mean?

God thereby tenderly encourages us to believe that He is truly our Father, and that we are truly His children, so that we may boldly and confidently come to Him in prayer, even as beloved children come to their dear father.

181. Why do we say "our" Father?

As Christians we do not pray each one for himself alone, but for one another. (See NOTES, 1. "I" Believe, and "Our" Father.)

This commandment have we from Him, that he who loveth God love his brother also. I John 4:21.

182. What have we become through faith in Jesus Christ?

We have become God's dear children and members of His household.

Ye are all the children of God by faith in Christ Jesus. Gal. 3:26.

Now therefore ye are no more strangers and foreigners, but fellow citizens with the saints, and of the household of God. Eph. 2:19.

(137)

183.   What should this encourage us to do?

> To come boldly and confidently to God in
> prayer. (See NOTES, 2. Prayer in the
> Christian Life.)

>> Casting all your care upon Him, for He
>> careth for you. I Pet. 5:7.
>> Let us therefore come boldly unto the throne
>> of grace, that we may obtain mercy, and find
>> grace to help in time of need. Heb. 4:16.
>> And this is the confidence that we have in
>> Him, that if we ask anything according to His
>> will, He heareth us. And if we know that He
>> hear us, whatsoever we ask, we know that we
>> have the petitions that we desired of Him. I
>> John 5:14, 15.

NOTES

1.   "I" BELIEVE, AND "OUR" FATHER.

In the Creed the pronouns referring to us are all sing-
ular: "*I* believe . . . . that God has made *me* . . . . that
Jesus Christ is *my* Lord," etc.   In the Lord's Prayer the
pronouns referring to us are all plural: "*Our* Father . . . .
give *us* this day . . . forgive *us* *our* trespasses." etc.   Each
one must believe for himself, but we can pray also for
others.   Not that any Christian would say, "I will let someone else do the praying for me."   Every Christian prays,
but not selfishly for himself alone.

2.   PRAYER IN THE CHRISTIAN LIFE.

Christians pray.   A life without prayer is not the Christian life.   James writes, "If any of you lack wisdom, let
him ask of God" (1:5); "ye have not because ye ask
not" (4:2); "draw nigh to God and He will draw nigh
to you" (4:8); "is any among you afflicted? let him pray"

(5:13) ; "the effectual fervent prayer of a righteous man availeth much" (5:16).

Every Christian should have a regular time and place for daily prayer, lest he neglect it. He is God's child, and he will not let a day pass without speaking to his Father.

We have a special promise that united prayer will be answered. "If two of you shall agree on earth as touching anything that they shall ask, it shall be done for them of my Father which is in heaven" (Matthew 18:19). Therefore Christians gladly join with others in prayer, as in family worship and congregational worship.

The work of the Christian Church is world wide, and often the individual Christian must live his life in one small area. Yet he can take part in Christian work everywhere by praying for the workers and the work. "Brethren, pray for us," wrote St. Paul to the Christians at Thessalonica (I Thessalonians 5:25).

SCRIPTURE READING

I John 3:1-10

FOR CLASS DISCUSSION

What would be the best time in the average household for family worship? What particular part of Christian work in the world would you like to share in through prayer? Do you think we should pray about national and international problems, who should be elected, who should win a war, etc.? Do you think the world would be better off if Christians prayed more?

PRAYER

We thank Thee, God that Thou art our Father through Jesus Christ, our Savior; and we pray that Thou wouldst keep us ever in the peace and joy of Thy household. Amen.

LESSON 29

THE FIRST PETITION

184. Which is the First Petition of the Lord's Prayer?

Hallowed be Thy name. (See NOTES, 1. Division of Petitions.)

185. What does this mean?

God's name is indeed holy in itself; but we pray in this petition that it may be hallowed also among us.

186. How is this done?

When the Word of God is taught in its truth and purity, and we, as God's children, lead holy lives in accordance with it. This grant us, dear Father in heaven! But whosoever teaches and lives otherwise than as God's Word teaches, profanes the name of God among us. From this preserve us, heavenly Father!

187. What do we pray for in this petition?

That God's name, Word and honor be held in respect by us and all men.

> Give unto the Lord the glory due unto His name. Ps. 96:8.
> Unto Him be glory in the Church by Christ Jesus throughout all ages, world without end. Eph. 3:21.

188.   When do we hallow God's name?

When we believe and teach the truth about
   God as He has revealed it in His Word,
   and live according to it. (SEE NOTES,
   2. Honoring God.)

> O worship the Lord in the beauty of holiness;
> fear before Him, all the earth. Say among the
> heathen that the Lord reigneth. Ps. 96:9, 10.

189.   When do we profane or dishonor God's name?

When we believe and teach otherwise than
   as God's Word teaches; or when we pretend to believe it and still do not live
   according to it.

> He that is of God heareth God's words. John
> 8:47.
> This people draweth nigh unto me with their
> mouth, and honoreth me with their lips; but
> their heart is far from me. Matthew 15:8.

NOTES

1.   DIVISION OF PETITIONS.

It has been noted that the first three petitions contain
the word "Thy" and the last four the word "us." It would
not be entirely correct, however, to say that the first three
ask for things pertaining to God, and the last four ask for
things pertaining to us. The first three also pertain to us,
and the blessings they ask are as important for us as the
blessings asked in the others.

The first four petitions are positive; they ask for the
bestowal of good things. The last three are negative; they
ask for the removal or warding off of the evil things; sins,
temptations, evil.

Of the first four, which ask for good things, only one — the fourth — asks for good things for the body. The petitions may thus be divided into 3, 1, 3.

1. Hallowed be Thy name
2. Thy kingdom come } For the bestowal of spiritual blessings.
3. Thy will be done

4. Give us this day.................For the bestowal of temporal blessings.

5. Forgive us
6. Lead us not } For protection against spiritual evils.
7. Deliver us

2. HONORING GOD.

To honor God we must first believe that He is. Atheists dishonor God.

We must also recognize His power and goodness. When the government stamps on its coins "In God We Trust," or calls upon people to worship God in their churches on Thanksgiving Day, it is a public recognition of God.

We must teach the truth about God. False teachers who teach lies in God's name dishonor Him.

We must obey His will. People who claim to be Christians, but who do not pray, do not go to church, do not love and help their fellow man, bring discredit and dishonor to the name of God.

SCRIPTURE READING
Psalm 96

FOR CLASS DISCUSSION

When we human beings pray, where are we most likely to put the emphasis? How does the Lord's Prayer differ from this?

The Second Commandment shows us some uses of God's name which dishonor Him. Name them. Other things that dishonor God: jokes that make fun of religion; work or pleasure that keeps people from church; a form of government that makes life harder for believers. What can you add to this list?

PRAYER

Let the people praise Thee, O God; let all the people praise Thee. Then shall the earth yield her increase; and God, even our own God, shall bless us. Amen. (Psalm 67:5, 6).

LESSON 30

THE SECOND PETITION

190. Which is the Second Petition?

Thy kingdom come.

191. What does this mean?

The kingdom of God comes indeed of itself, without our prayer; but we pray in this petition that it may also come to us.

192. How is this done?

When our heavenly Father gives us His Holy Spirit, so that by His grace we believe His holy Word, and live a godly life here on earth, and in heaven forever.

> Except a man be born of water and of the Spirit, he cannot enter into the kingdom of God. John 3:5.

193. What do we pray for in this petition?

That God may rule in the hearts and lives of of ourselves and all men. (See NOTES, 1. Kingdom of God.)

> Be still, and know that I am God. I will be exalted among the heathen; I will be exalted in the earth. Ps. 46:10.
> Behold, the kingdom of God is within you. Luke 17:21.

194. Can we bring this to pass by ourselves?

We cannot; therefore we pray that God may give us His Holy Spirit.

(144)

> If ye then, being evil, know how to give good
> gifts unto your children, how much more shall
> your heavenly Father give the Holy Spirit to
> them that ask Him? Luke 11:13.

195.   What can we do to help God's kingdom come?

We can bear faithful witness to Him by our
words and our lives. (See NOTES, 2.
Missions.)

> This Gospel of the kingdom shall be preached
> in all the world for a witness unto all nations.
> Matthew 24:14.
> Ye shall be witnesses unto me. Acts 1:8.

NOTES

1.   KINGDOM OF GOD.

God is the ruler over all things, whether we wish it or
not. His will must triumph in the end, whether we help
bring it to pass or not. Therefore Luther says that the
kingdom of God "comes of itself without our prayer."

That does not mean that Christians may pray or not
pray, work or not work for the coming of the kingdom,
as they see fit. If we are not interested, God will accomplish His purposes through others; but it will make a great
difference to us and to others who might have been reached
through us.

But Christians *are* interested. They are God's children
and His will is their will. They can think of no happier
state of affairs than that which would exist if God ruled
the lives of themselves, their friends, their neighbors and
all human beings. They want (as God wants) their neighbors to be in the kingdom of grace through faith in Christ
Jesus, and thus to reach the kingdom of glory. Therefore
they pray and work for the coming of the kingdom.

2. MISSIONS.

One way in which the Church is commanded to help God's kingdom come is through Christian missions.

The word "mission" comes from the Latin "mitto," which means "I send." God sends the Church out to bear witness. "Go ye therefore and make disciples of all nations" (Matthew 28:19). "Go ye into all the world and preach the Gospel to every creature" (Mark 16:15). No Christian is excused from obeying this command. Every Christian is to be a missionary.

In order to send missionaries to far heathen countries, Christians join together in large groups to share the expense. Such mission work is called Foreign Missions. Our own American Lutheran Church is doing such work in India and in New Guinea.

Mission work that is done in our own land is called Home Missions. Every congregation should do home mission work in its community.

Mission work that combines kindness to prisoners, the sick, the unfortunate with its witnessing for Christ is called Inner Missions.

There are also various special missions which derive their name from the group they are intended to reach, such as Negro Missions, Jewish Missions, Mexican Missions.

SCRIPTURE READING

Acts 1:1-8

FOR CLASS DISCUSSION

Do you want God's kingdom to come? What advantages do you think would follow, if the kingdom of God came to your town? What things do you think would be different from the present condition? What things would be missing? What would be present that is not present now? Does God want His kingdom to come to your community? If enough people wanted God's kingdom to come to your town, do you think it would come? What can you do to help it come?

PRAYER

Thy kingdom come, O God. Rule in my heart and speak through my tongue, that others also may be brought under Thy kindly rule, and Thy kingdom come. Amen.

LESSON 31

THE THIRD PETITION

196. Which is the Third Petition of the Lord's Prayer?

Thy will be done on earth, as it is in heaven.

197. What does this mean?

The good and gracious will of God is done indeed without our prayer; but we pray in this petition that it may also be done among us.

198. How is this done?

When God destroys and brings to naught every evil counsel and purpose of the devil, the world, and our own flesh, which would hinder us from hallowing His name, and prevent the coming of His kingdom; and when He strengthens us and keeps us steadfast in His Word and in faith, even unto our end. This is His good and gracious will.

199. What do we pray for in this petition?

That God would help us to do His will as perfectly as the angels in heaven; and to that end would oppose and destroy every evil will. (See NOTES, 1. The First Three Petitions.)

Teach me to do Thy will, for Thou art my God. Ps. 143:10.

Not everyone that saith unto me, Lord, Lord, shall enter into the kingdom of heaven; but he that doeth the will of my Father which is in heaven. Matthew 7:21.

200. Who has such an evil will?

The devil. (See NOTES, 2. Satan.)

The world. (The world of unbelievers.)

Our own flesh. (Our sinful nature.)

Love not the world, neither the things that are in the world. If any man love the world, the love of the Father is not in him. For all that is in the world, the lust of the flesh, and the lust of the eyes, and the pride of life, is not of the Father but is of the world. And the world passeth away, and the lust thereof; but he that doeth the will of God abideth forever. I John 2:15-17.

201. How does God help us to do His will?

Through His Holy Spirit He gives us grace to continue steadfast in His Word and in faith. (See NOTES, 3. Doing God's Will.)

It is God which worketh in you both to will and to do of His good pleasure. Phil. 2:13.

When He, the Spirit of truth, is come, He will guide you into all truth. John 16:13.

NOTES

1. THE FIRST THREE PETITIONS.

These three petitions are closely related to one another. They deal with God's name, God's kingdom, God's will. Those who hallow God's name will also work for the coming of His kingdom and do His will. We cannot do God's will without working for the coming of His kingdom, for that is His will. If we hallow God's name we are doing God's will, for He wants men to respect and honor Him and His truth. If we do not do His will, we are not hallowing His name, but dishonoring it.' The three petitions get at the same thing in three ways: that we should respect and obey God as the King of our lives.

2. SATAN.

Satan, or the devil, is the leader of the fallen angels who rebelled against God and now oppose His will. He is also called the prince of this world, the ruler of darkness, the tempter, the wicked one, the father of lies, the adversary, the accuser.

3. DOING GOD'S WILL.

It is not enough to *know* God's will; we must also *do* it. In the Ten Commandments we learned some of the things God wants us to do and not to do. In the Creed we learned that we cannot become God's children through faith in Christ unless the Holy Spirit leads us. Even after we are God's people the Spirit continues to sanctify us, that is, He gives us grace to do God's will. When in the Lord's Prayer we ask that God's will be done, we mean that God the Holy Spirit should continue to sanctify us, that is, that He should help us and all men to understand God's Word, believe it, and do it.

SCRIPTURE READING
Matthew 26:36-46

FOR CLASS DISCUSSION

Suppose a workman is told by his boss to go on working, but is ordered by his union leader to go on strike. Here is a clash of wills. When two wills are opposite, can both be done? What must happen? Where only is there a will? In a mountain or river or field? In a house or machine? Where only? Besides your own will, then, what other wills can urge you to action? Of all these wills which is supreme? If there is a clash between wills, how do we know what we ought to do?

PRAYER

Teach me to do Thy will, for Thou art my God. When my own will or other wills tempt me to disobey Thee, help me to remember that the will of my Father is always best for me. Thy will be done. Amen.

LESSON 32

THE FOURTH PETITION

202. Which is the Fourth Petition?

Give us this day our daily bread.

203. What does this mean?

God indeed gives daily bread to all men, even to the wicked, without our prayer; but we pray in this petition that He would lead us to acknowledge our daily bread as His gift, and to receive it with thanksgiving.

204. What is meant by daily bread?

Everything that is required to satisfy our bodily needs: such as food and raiment, house and home, fields and flocks, money and goods; pious parents, children and servants; godly and faithful rulers, good government; seasonable weather, peace and health; order and honor; true friends, good neighbors, and the like.

205. What do we pray for in this petition?

For our daily bread, that is, for everything that we need for our bodily life. (See NOTES, 1. Needs of the Body.)

> Every good gift and every perfect gift is from above, and cometh down from the Father of lights. James 1:17.

206. If God gives bread to all men, why do we pray for it?

> We thus hallow His name by acknowledging Him as the giver.

>> He maketh His sun to rise on the evil and on the good and sendeth rain on the just and on the unjust. Matthew 5:45.

207. Why do we pray for "this day" only?

> Because we trust in God and we are not anxiously concerned for the morrow. (See NOTES, 2. Worry.)

>> Take therefore no thought for the morrow, for the morrow will take thought for the things of itself. Sufficient unto the day is the evil thereof. Matthew 6:34.
>>
>> Behold the fowls of the air, for they sow not, neither do they reap nor gather into barns; yet your heavenly Father feedeth them. Are ye not much better than they? Matthew 6:26.

NOTES

1. NEEDS OF THE BODY.

After three petitions that ask for spiritual blessings, Jesus sums up all needs of the body in one petition. It names bread as representing the whole class of things the body needs. Water and air are as necessary to the body as food.

Luther explained the petition for his time and people. Many of us today do not have "fields and flocks," but the fields and flocks must exist somewhere if we are to live.

Can you explain how the other things Luther mentions —pious parents, good government, etc.— are necessary to life?

In many ways life has changed since Luther's time. Today we need factories and machines, and we need the chance to work at our jobs, free from depressions and strikes.

The knowledge of the proper care of the body has also increased since Luther's time. Medicines that are very helpful in saving and prolonging life have been discovered, also preventives like typhoid and tetanus antitoxins. We know of the germ-killing action of sun light, and of the need for certain elements in our food (vitamins). All these are gifts of God, by which our life and health are maintained.

2. WORRY.

When Jesus says, "Take no thought for the morrow," He does not mean that we are not to plan for future needs. For in the same place He speaks of birds and says that they do not sow or reap. By that He recognizes that men *do* sow and reap. And every time a man sows seed he is planning for future needs.

The Lord means that we are not to be *anxious* about the future. We are not to worry. For worry is the opposite of trusting in God. (See Questions 24 and 109 and the Notes to Lesson 16.) Christians trust in God who is their Father. Tomorrow they will pray again, so today they pray only for the needs of today. God will still be here tomorrow.

SCRIPTURE READING

Psalm 104

FOR CLASS DISCUSSION

Have you had an operation? Not so many years ago it would not have been possible. God lets us discover more helps for the body as we find more foolish ways of injuring it. What common cause of death can you mention that was not known in Luther's day? How else do modern living conditions endanger life? How do improved means of transportation contribute to health?

PRAYER

Father, we thank Thee for this food and for all the blessings which Thou dost bestow upon us. May this bread sustain our bodies, and Thy Word, the bread of life, sustain our souls unto everlasting life. Amen.

LESSON 33

THE FIFTH PETITION

208. Which is the Fifth Petition?

And forgive us our trespasses, as we forgive those who trespass against us.

209. What does this mean?

We pray in this petition that our heavenly Father would not regard our sins, nor because of them deny our prayers; for we neither merit, nor deserve those things for which we pray; but that He would grant us all things through grace, even though we sin daily, and deserve nothing but punishment. And certainly we, on our part, will heartily forgive and gladly do good to those who may sin against us.

210. What do we pray for in this petition?

That God would not remember our sins against us; for if they were not forgiven we could expect nothing but punishment. (See NOTES, 1. Forgiveness of Sins.)

The wages of sin is death; but the gift of God is eternal life through Jesus Christ our Lord. Rom. 6:23.

(156)

> If Thou, Lord, shouldst mark iniquities, O Lord, who shall stand? But there is forgiveness with Thee, that Thou mayest be feared. Ps. 130:3, 4.
>
> As far as the east is from the west, so far hath He removed our transgressions from us. Ps. 103:12.

211. Why does God forgive our sins?

He does it for Christ's sake. (See Question 163.)

> God hath made Him to be sin for us who knew no sin, that we might be made the righteousness of God in Him. II Cor. 5:21.

212. When may we expect forgiveness of God?

When we as His children forgive others as He forgives us. (See NOTES, 2. The Forgiving Spirit.)

> If ye forgive not men their trespasses, neither will your Father forgive your trespasses. Matthew 6:15.

NOTES

1. THE FORGIVENESS OF SINS

In the Second Article of the Creed we learned that Christ has redeemed us from all sins. (See Questions 127 and 132.)

In the Third Article we confess, "I believe the forgiveness of sins." The explanation of that Article says that in the Christian Church God "daily forgives abundantly all my sins and the sins of all believers." (See Lesson 25.)

Here in the Lord's Prayer we come upon the forgiveness of sins again. We shall also find the same subject spoken of in connection with Baptism, Confession and the Office of the Keys, and the Lord's Supper.

It occurs so often because the forgiveness of sins is the very heart of the Christian religion. Christ died for us, and therefore our sins are forgiven if we believe in Him. This is justification by faith. (See Note 1, Lesson 25.)

2. THE FORGIVING SPIRIT.

God forgives us daily and abundantly. We live in an atmosphere of forgiveness. It is not like our partaking of water, which we drink, and presently we are thirsty again and need another drink. It is more like the air around us, which we breathe constantly. It is like the sunlight, which is always shining on our earth. As long as we are in Christ Jesus, forgiveness is constantly, continuously ours, flowing from God to us in an uninterrupted stream, as light radiates from the sun.

God forgives us because it is His nature to forgive. If we are God's children, we shall be like Him, and it will also be our nature to forgive. If we are not willing to forgive those who sin against us, it shows that we are not like God. Christians cannot be hateful, unforgiving, holding grudges.

If we pray the Lord's Prayer and do not forgive others, we really are asking God *not* to forgive us, for we say, "Forgive . . . . as we forgive."

SCRIPTURE READING

Matthew 18:21-35

FOR CLASS DISCUSSION

Should we forgive even wicked people, or only our fellow Christians? Does God forgive sinners or righteous people? If we were without sin, could God forgive us?

If we forgive transgressors should we also remit the penalty of their transgressions? Does God love sin when He loves the sinner? Suppose a man breaks God's laws for the body (drinks too much, etc.) until he has ruined his health. Suppose he then repents and asks forgiveness for Jesus' sake. Will God forgive him? But will that give him a new body? If a criminal repents and is forgiven, will he want to finish his term in jail, or will he want to be excused from the punishment?

PRAYER

For Jesus' sake forgive me all the sins which I have this day committed, and help me to lie down to sleep forgiving all those who have sinned against me. Amen.

LESSON 34

THE SIXTH PETITION

213. Which is the Sixth Petition?

And lead us not into temptation.

214. What does this mean?

God indeed tempts no one to sin; but we pray in this petition that God would so guard and preserve us, that the devil, the world, and our own flesh may not deceive us, nor lead us into error and unbelief, despair, and other great and shameful sins; but that, when so tempted, we may finally prevail and gain the victory.

Let no man say when he is tempted, I am tempted of God; for God cannot be tempted with evil, neither tempteth He any man. But every man is tempted when he is drawn away of his own lust, and enticed. James 1:13, 14.

215. What do we pray for in this petition?

That God would keep us from being tempted by the devil, the world, and our own flesh (see Question 200) ; and that if we are tempted He would keep us from yielding to the temptation. (See NOTES, 1. Temptations.)

How can I do this great wickedness, and sin against God? Gen. 39:9.

216.   What are some of the great sins from which we pray
       to be delivered?

   Error (wrong belief).
   Unbelief (not to believe God at all).
   Despair (to lose hope in God).

217.   How can we resist temptation?

   By remaining in constant touch with God
       through His Word and through our
       prayer. (See NOTES, 2. Resisting Temp-
       tation.)

   **Resist the devil and he will flee from you.
   James 4:7.**
   **Watch and pray that ye enter not into tempta-
   tion. Matthew 26:41.**

NOTES

1.   TEMPTATIONS.

Sometimes the word "tempt" is used in the broad
sense of "to try," that is, to test a person in order to see
what he will do under certain circumstances. "God did
tempt Abraham" (Genesis 22:1).

Usually, however, the word "tempt" means to try to
get someone to go against God's will. Satan is the great
tempter. (See Matthew 4:1-11.)

Some temptations come through the needs of the body,
as the temptation to steal when one is hungry. Some are
direct temptations of the spirit, as temptations to pride,
unbelief, despair. All of them aim to produce sin, to get
a soul to disobey God, and thus bring about a separation
of the soul from God.

2.   RESISTING TEMPTATION.

One thing we can do to resist temptation is to avoid
places and company where temptation is likely to occur.

"My son, walk not thou in the way with them" (Proverbs 1:15).

A strong faith in God is good defensive armor against temptation. "Above all, taking the shield of faith, wherewith ye shall be able to quench all the fiery darts of the wicked." (Ephesians 6:16. Read also verses 10-18.)

Jesus showed us how to answer the temptations of the evil one with the Word of God (Matthew 4:1-11).

If, when we are tempted, we immediately turn to God in prayer, the temptation will lose its force and presently disappear. "God is faithful, who will not suffer you to be tempted above that ye are able; but will with the temptation also make a way to escape, that ye may be able to bear it" (I Corinthians 10:13).

SCRIPTURE READING
Matthew 4:1-11

FOR CLASS DISCUSSION

How are children tempted most frequently? Name some places you think Christians should avoid in order to stay away from temptation. What kind of company should be avoided?

Can God be tempted to do evil? If two of you were together, and one were tempted but the other were not, would there be as much likelihood of the tempted one yielding to sin as if he were alone? What companion can we always have with us to make us stronger against temptation?

PRAYER

Lord Jesus, be with me today wherever I go, and let no evil thought arise in my mind. But if I am tempted, help me to remember that Thou art with me, and to turn to Thee for help. Amen.

LESSON 35

THE SEVENTH PETITION

218. Which is the Seventh Petition?

But deliver us from evil.

219. What does this mean?

We pray in this petition, as in a summary, that our heavenly Father would deliver us from all manner of evil, whether it affect the body or soul, property or reputation, and at last, when the hour of death shall come, grant us a blessed end, and graciously take us from this world of sorrow to Himself in heaven.

He shall deliver thee in six troubles; yea, in seven there shall no evil touch thee. Job 5:19.

220. What do we pray for in this petition?

That God would save us from every harm to body or soul, property or reputation. (See Notes, 1. Evils.)

Call upon me in the day of trouble; I will deliver thee, and thou shalt glorify me. Ps. 50:15.

221. What is the greatest deliverance from evil?

When God finally delivers us from all evil by granting us a blessed end and taking us to Himself in heaven.

> Blessed are the dead which die in the Lord. Rev. 14:13.
>
> In Thy presence is fulness of joy; at Thy right hand there are pleasures for evermore. Ps. 16:11.
>
> God shall wipe away all tears from their eyes; and there shall be no more death, neither sorrow nor crying, neither shall there be any more pain. Rev. 21:4.

NOTES

1. EVILS.

When we pray, "Deliver us from evil," we should not forget that we have prayed the earlier petition, "Thy will be done." In the garden of Gethsemane Jesus prayed, "Let this cup pass from me." That was a prayer for deliverance from evil. But He added, "Nevertheless not as I will but as Thou wilt" (Matthew 26:39). And since it was God's will that He should suffer and die, Jesus was not delivered from that evil.

It would not be best for us if we lived a life of perfect ease and happiness. Pain, for example, is often a signal that something is wrong with the body and should be attended to. Without that signal we might rush into greater evils without knowing it.

Loss of property is an evil. But sometimes the only way God can wake a man up to more important things is by causing him to lose his earthly wealth. When Jesus told the rich young ruler (Mark 10:17-22) to sell all that he had and give the proceeds to the poor, it was kindly advice and meant for the young man's good.

Since sin has entered the world, bringing with it sickness and sorrow and death, we cannot expect to avoid all unpleasant experiences. But we know that God can turn even unpleasant things into blessings (see Note 4, Lesson

16), and make "all things work together for good to them that love God" (Romans 8:28).

What we are praying for is that we be delivered from evils *in accordance with God's will.* If it is His will that we suffer, the suffering will turn out to be a blessing. Read Hebrews 12:9-11.

SCRIPTURE READING

Psalm 91

FOR CLASS DISCUSSION

Should we pray to God to keep us from ever having any sorrow at all? Give reasons for your answer. Why did God not deliver His own Son from sorrow and pain? What does that prove regarding His will for us? Read Romans 8:32. Who has an evil will toward us? May we pray for deliverance from all the sorrows that this evil will would bring upon us? If God sends us sorrow is it an evil?

PRAYER

Dear Father, Thy will be done. Keep us from all harm and danger according to Thy good will; and if Thy goodness sends us sorrow, help us obtain the blessing from it which Thou dost intend. Amen.

LESSON 36

THE CONCLUSION

222. What is the Conclusion of the Lord's Prayer?

For Thine is the kingdom, and the power, and the glory, forever and ever. Amen.

223. What does this mean?

That all things are under God's rule.

That He can do whatsoever He will.

That all things must work out to His honor and praise.

> He ruleth by His power forever. Ps. 66:7.
>
> We give Thee thanks, O Lord God Almighty, which art and wast and art to come, because Thou hast taken to Thee Thy great power and hast reigned. Rev. 11:17.

224. What does the word "Amen" mean?

It means that I should be assured that such petitions are acceptable to our heavenly Father, and are heard by Him; for He Himself has commanded us to pray in this manner, and has promised to hear us. Amen, Amen, that is, Yea, yea, it shall be so. (See NOTES, 1. Amen.)

> And this is the confidence that we have in Him, that if we ask anything according to His will, He heareth us. And if we know that He hear us, whatsoever we ask, we know that we have the petitions that we desired of Him. I John 5:14, 15.

225. Does God always answer believing prayer?

> Yes, in His own good time, and according
> to His perfect wisdom. (See NOTES, 2.
> Answers to Prayer.)

>> I sought the Lord and He heard me, and
>> delivered me from all my fears. Ps. 34:4.

NOTES

1. AMEN.

The word "Amen" has come down to us from Bible
times unchanged. It has entered all modern languages
without being translated. It means "verily" or "truly."
So that "Amen" at the end of a prayer is in itself a prayer
(may it truly be so), and a confession of faith (I believe
that it shall truly be so, as I have prayed).

2. ANSWERS TO PRAYER.

We have God's promise, repeated over and over again
in the Bible, that the prayers of His people will be heard
and answered.

However, we should not lose faith if our prayers are
apparently not heard. Our wisdom is so limited that
sometimes we ask for things it would not be good for us
to have. Then God gives us a different and better answer
to our prayer than the one we hoped for. For example,
if one is suffering from some bodily ailment, and prays
for health, God may instead give him patience and courage
to bear his affliction, and thus make him a stronger char-
acter and an example to others. Read II Corinthians
12:7-10.

Or the answer to prayer may be delayed in the wisdom
of God. We must be content to wait on the Lord's good
time. All through the Old Testament times there were
godly people who prayed for the coming of the promised

Savior. But when the fulness of time was come, God sent
forth His Son (Galatians 4:4) — not before.

SCRIPTURE READING

Revelation 7:9-17

FOR CLASS DISCUSSION

Suppose half the Christians in the country prayed for
one candidate for president to win the election, and the
other half prayed just as earnestly for the other candidate.
Could God answer both sets of prayers? Should we then
not pray for such things as elections? If we have prayed
for the success of one candidate, and the other wins, what
should we think about it? If a group of Christians met
just before election time, some of them believing in the
principles of one party and others believing in the principles of a different party, could those Christians pray together about the election? Tell what you think ought
to be said in their prayer.

PRAYER

Verily, God hath heard me; He hath attended to the
voice of my prayer. Blessed be God, which hath not turned
away my prayer, nor His mercy from me. Amen. (Psalm
66:19, 20).

PART IV

BAPTISM

THE BAPTISM OF JESUS

LESSON 37

WHAT BAPTISM IS

226. What is Baptism?

Baptism is not simply water, but it is the water used according to God's command and connected with God's Word. (See NOTES, 1. Sacraments.)

227. How is a person baptized?

Water is applied in the name of the Father and of the Son and of the Holy Ghost.

> See, here is water; what doth hinder me to be baptized? Acts 8:36.

228. Who baptizes?

As a rule the ministers of the Church; but in case of emergency any confirmed Christian may baptize. (A form for baptism in cases of necessity is found in our Hymnal.)

229. Who should be baptized?

All who are to be brought to the Lord Jesus as His disciples.

> Ye are all the children of God by faith in Christ Jesus. For as many of you as have been baptized into Christ have put on Christ. Gal. 3:26, 27.
> Except a man be born of water and of the Spirit, he cannot enter into the kingdom of God. John 3:5.

230.   Where is this written?

In the Word of command connected with
Baptism.

231.   What is this Word of command?

*It is the Word of our Lord Jesus Christ, as
recorded in the last chapter of Matthew:
"Go ye therefore, and make disciples of
all the nations, baptizing them in the
name of the Father, and of the Son, and
of the Holy Ghost."*

1.   SACRAMENTS.   **NOTES**

Baptism is one of the two New Testament sacraments,
the other being the Lord's Supper.

A sacrament is a holy rite, instituted by Christ, whereby
the treasures of the Gospel (forgiveness of sins, life and
salvation) are offered, given and sealed unto us under a
visible element. The sacraments offer us the same treasures
offered by the Word of God, with this difference: in a
sacrament a visible element is added as a sign and seal of
God's promise of forgiveness, strengthening our weak
faith.

The Roman Catholic Church teaches that there are
seven sacraments: Baptism, Confirmation, Ordination, Marriage, Confession, the Lord's Supper, and Extreme Unction.
Only two of these have all the characteristics of a sacrament.

2.   BAPTISM OF CHILDREN.

There are groups, such as the Baptists, who do not believe in baptizing small children.

They say, Children cannot believe. We reply, Neither
can grown persons, of their own reason or strength. "No

man can say that Jesus is the Lord but by the Holy Ghost"
(I Corinthians 12:3). If the Holy Ghost must produce
this faith in us, why can He not produce it in the infant
soul; and the more readily because that soul is not yet
hardened in habits of sin?

They cannot deny the possibility of the Holy Spirit
working in the heart of a child, for the Bible says that John
the Baptist was filled with the Holy Ghost even before
his birth. Luke 1:15.

They cannot deny that children are born sinners and
need regeneration. See John 3:6; Psalm 51:5; Ephesians
2:3. Nor can they deny that Jesus wants the children.
Mark 10:14. We ask, How else can little children be
brought to God? They cannot understand the preaching
of the Gospel, and they cannot receive the Lord's Supper
until they are able to examine themselves. I Corinthians
11:28. The only means of grace open to them is the sacrament of Baptism.

The baptismal command includes "all nations," of
which the children form a large percentage. In the Old
Testament male children were brought into covenant rela-
tionship with God at the age of eight days, and that by
the command of God. The apostles baptized entire house-
holds: Acts 16:15 and 33; I Corinthians 1:16. The apostles
wrote to children as to Christians: Ephesians 6:1; I John
2:12. We know that the early Church, in the centuries
following the apostles, practiced infant baptism.

3. SPONSORS.

When infants are baptized, it is with the expectation
that they will be brought up as Christians. The baptismal
command says that all nations are to be made disciples,
and adds two words as to how that is to be done: "Baptizing" and "Teaching." Nothing is said as to which is to
come first. Common sense indicates that grown persons

should be taught first and then baptized; infants baptized first and then taught. Sponsors are persons who make the responses for infants in baptism, renouncing the devil and all his works and ways, confessing the Christian faith, and promising that the child shall be brought up in this faith.

This is first of all the duty of Christian parents. But when the Church was suffering persecution, parents could not be sure that they would live long enough to see to the Christian training of their children. So they would ask others to promise to look after it, in case the parents themselves were killed or imprisoned. Sponsors are most necessary in times of danger to the Church.

SCRIPTURE READING

Acts 8:26-40

FOR CLASS DISCUSSION

Are you a Christian? Why? Can you remember a time when you were not a believer in Christ? If you have been a believer as long as you can remember, you must have become a believer before reason and memory were active. Who created that faith in your infant heart? Who always creates faith? Then you know by experience that the Holy Spirit creates faith in the infant soul, do you not?

PRAYER

Father, I thank Thee that Thou didst receive me as Thy child in Baptism, causing me to be born again of water and the Spirit. Amen.

LESSON 38

THE BENEFIT OF BAPTISM

232. What gifts or benefits does Baptism bestow?

It works forgiveness of sins, delivers from death and the devil, and gives everlasting salvation to all who believe, as the Word and promise of God declare.

233. What is this Word and promise of God?

It is the Word of our Lord Jesus Christ, as recorded in the last chapter of Mark: "He that believeth and is baptized shall be saved; but he that believeth not shall be damned."

234. What does Baptism work?

It works forgiveness of sins. (See NOTES, 1. Baptismal Regeneration.)

> Repent, and be baptized every one of you in the name of Jesus Christ for the remission of sins. Acts 2:38.
>
> And now why tarriest thou? Arise and be baptized, and wash away thy sins, calling on the name of the Lord. Acts. 22:16.

235. By working forgiveness of sins, what else does Baptism do for us?

It delivers from death and the devil, and gives everlasting salvation.

> Know ye not that so many of us as were baptized into Jesus Christ were baptized into His death? Rom. 6:3.

(175)

> Forasmuch then as the children are partakers of flesh and blood, He also Himself likewise took part of the same; that through death He might destroy him that had the power of death, that is, the devil, and deliver them who through fear of death were all their lifetime subject to bondage. Heb. 2:14, 15.

236.   Who receives these blessings of Baptism?

He that believeth and is baptized. (See Notes, 2. Faith and the Sacraments.)

NOTES

1. Baptismal Regeneration.

Regeneration means rebirth, being born again. "Ye must be born again" (John 3:7).

Regeneration is the work of the Holy Spirit, and takes place when a sinner is brought to Christ in faith and thus is made a child of God. Regeneration, faith, sonship, and forgiveness or justification all occur together.

We have seen that Baptism has the promise of the forgiveness of sins. See Acts 2:38 and 22:16, Question 234. Where forgiveness of sin is, there is also life and salvation. Therefore we believe in baptismal regeneration, that is, that children who are born in sin are reborn in baptism. Baptism is to us a sacrament which gives the treasures of the Gospel. In the case of grown persons, regeneration takes place through hearing the Word of God, and Baptism then follows.

The Baptist groups who do not believe in the Baptism of infants do not believe in baptismal regeneration. They hold to the Baptism of believers, and insist on Baptism by immersion. They do not speak of sacraments, but call Baptism an "ordinance." It is strange that those who make so much of the *method* of Baptism should make so little of its *content*.

2.   FAITH AND THE SACRAMENTS.

A sacrament is a sacrament whether we believe in it or not. "What if some did not believe? Shall their unbelief make the faith (faithfulness, R. V.) of God without effect?" (Romans 3:3). But if we are to get any benefit of a sacrament, we must believe.

In the case of an infant, faith is created in Baptism, even though the child is not conscious of it; and that faith lays hold on the benefit of Baptism, and continues to live and grow until it becomes a conscious faith.

Notice that Jesus did not say, "He that is not baptized shall be damned," but only, "He that believeth not." A man could be saved by faith alone, without Baptism, if only he had not despised Baptism.

SCRIPTURE READING

Acts 16:19-34

FOR CLASS DISCUSSION

Suppose an unbeliever were marooned alone on a desert island with a Bible. Through reading the Bible he came to believe in Jesus, but there was no one to baptize him. Would he be a Christian? But if he were rescued from the island, what would he want to do? If he believed in Christ through the influence of the Spirit in the Word, did he have the treasures of the Gospel? Could Baptism add anything to that? What?

PRAYER

Holy Spirit, who hast caused us to be born again of water and the Word, preserve and strengthen the faith there committed unto us, and keep us in that faith unto the end. Amen.

LESSON 39

HOW BAPTISM CONFERS ITS BENEFITS

237. How can water do such great things?

It is not the water, indeed, that does such great things, but the Word of God connected with the water, and our faith which relies on that Word of God. For without the Word of God, it is simply water and no Baptism. But when connected with the Word of God, it is a Baptism, that is, a gracious water of life and a washing of regeneration in the Holy Ghost, as St. Paul says to Titus, in the third chapter:

"According to His mercy He saved us, by the washing of regeneration, and renewing of the Holy Ghost; which He shed on us abundantly through Jesus Christ, our Savior; that, being justified by His grace, we should be made heirs according to the hope of eternal life. This is a faithful saying."

238. What gives Baptism its power?

It is not the water indeed that does such great things, but the Word of God connected with the water, and our faith which relies on that Word of God. (See Notes, 1. The Water in Baptism.)

239.   What does the Word of God say of Baptism?

That it is a gracious water of life and a washing of regeneration in the Holy Ghost.

> Christ loved the Church and gave Himself for it, that He might sanctify and cleanse it with the washing of water by the Word. Eph. 5:25, 26.
>
> Have ye received the Holy Ghost since ye believed? And they said unto him, We have not so much as heard whether there be any Holy Ghost. And He said unto them, Unto what then were ye baptized? Acts 19:2, 3.
>
> Repent, and be baptized every one of you in the name of Jesus Christ for the remission of sins, and ye shall receive the gift of the Holy Ghost. Acts 2:38.

NOTES

1.   THE WATER IN BAPTISM.

Baptists say that the word "baptism" means immersion only, and that only immersion (being submerged under the water) is baptism. They hold that we who have been baptized by sprinkling have not been truly baptized; and if one of us wanted to join a Baptist congregation, he would have to be rebaptized by immersion.

We believe that the amount of water used has nothing to do with the value of the sacrament. It is a sacrament, that is, a rite in which spiritual benefits are given by means of an earthly and visible element. The spiritual benefits are the important thing, and they are not dependent on the amount of water used, but on the Word of the Lord. "It is not water indeed that does such great things, but Word of God connected with the water."

We do not say that immersion is not a Baptism. If a Christian who had been baptized by immersion wanted to join one of our churches, he would not be rebaptized.

The word "baptism" as used in the New Testament means any washing of purification, not necessarily immersions. Mark 7:4; Luke 11:38; Heb. 9:10.

The early Church knew a "Baptism of the sick-bed," that is, the baptizing of people too sick to get up. This was certainly not immersion.

Pictures of Baptism in the catacombs under the city of Rome, whither the Christians were driven by persecutions of the Roman emperors (before 325 A. D.) show the rite being performed by pouring.

All nations are to be baptized; but immersion would not be practicable in very cold countries.

The water used in Baptism should be clean water. Whether it is well or cistern water, flowing or still water makes no difference.

SCRIPTURE READING

Acts 21:39; 22:16

FOR CLASS DISCUSSION

Read I Corinthians 10:2. Then read Exodus 14, especially verses 16 and 29. St. Paul says, "Our fathers were all baptized (unto Moses) in the sea." Were they immersed? Who were immersed? When Moses held out his rod over the sea and the sea divided, was it his rod that did such great things? Who did it? Does God have to have much water to cleanse a soul of sin?

PRAYER

Father, we thank Thee for Thy Word, which unites itself with such a simple thing as water and makes it for us a sacrament of regeneration. Amen.

LESSON 40

WHAT BAPTISM SIGNIFIES

240.   What does such baptizing with water signify?

It signifies that the old Adam in us, together with all sins and evil lusts, should be drowned by daily sorrow and repentance, and be put to death; and that the new man should daily come forth and rise, to live before God in righteousness and holiness forever.

241.   Where is it so written?

St. Paul, in the sixth chapter of the Epistle to the Romans, says: "We are buried with Christ by Baptism into death, that like as He was raised up from the dead by the glory of the Father, even so we also should walk in newness of life."

242.   Of what is the water of Baptism a sign?

Of the death and burial of the old Adam in us (our sinful nature, inherited from Adam). (See NOTES, 1. Burial by Baptism.)

> That ye put off concerning the former conversation the old man, which is corrupt according to the deceitful lusts. Eph. 4:22.

243.   How is the old Adam in us to be put to death?

By daily sorrow and repentance.

Our old man is crucified with Him, that the body of sin might be destroyed, that henceforth we should not serve sin. Rom. 6:6.

244. What is to follow the new birth of Baptism?

The new man should daily come forth and rise, to live before God in righteousness and holiness forever. (See NOTES, 2. Confirmation, and 3. Growing in Grace.)

And that ye put on the new man, which after God is created in righteousness and true holiness. Eph. 4:24.

Grow in grace, and in the knowledge of our Lord and Savior Jesus Christ. II Peter 3:18.

NOTES

1. BURIAL BY BAPTISM.

Immersionists use the passage in Romans 6, "We are buried with Christ by Baptism into death," to prove that Baptism should be by immersion, which "buries" the body under the water. They fail to see that St. Paul is here using figurative language. If the words "buried with Christ" are to be taken literally as referring to the body, then the other two words, "into death," will also have to be understood literally of the body, which would make every Baptism a drowning. Luther rightly points out that it is not the body which is to be buried and drowned, but the old Adam.

2. CONFIRMATION.

In the Lutheran Church, children who were baptized as infants are taught the truths of God's Word when they have reached the proper age to understand them, and are then confirmed. With us confirmation is not a sacrament as it is with the Roman Catholics, for it was not instituted by Christ, and there is no promise of God that He will bestow grace by it. It is a sacred churchly ceremony, wherein those who were baptized as infants publicly make for themselves the promises that were made for them by their sponsors at Baptism, and in which the prayers of the Church are offered to God for these young people.

Confirmed young people, having been thoroughly instructed in the Christian faith and life, are thereafter admitted to the sacrament of the Lord's Supper, and may also act as sponsors for children in Baptism.

3. GROWING IN GRACE.

Confirmation does not mean that we have reached the highest point in our Christian life, or have been made perfect. We sin daily (See Question 209) and need to repent daily. As long as we live we should continue to grow in grace, learning more and more by the help of the Holy Spirit to know God's will and to do it. See Notes, Good Works (Lesson 23), and Doing God's Will (Lesson 31).

SCRIPTURE READING
Romans 6:1-11

FOR CLASS DISCUSSION
When a seed is planted and the plant comes up, what does it do? If a child did not grow could it live? Can the new life implanted in us at Baptism continue as it should, if it does not grow? What is necessary for physical growth? Can you name the corresponding things that are necessary for spiritual growth? See John 6:48 and I Timothy 4:8.

PRAYER
Help us, O Lord, to grow in grace; that we may more and more hate and forsake all things displeasing to Thee, and more and more love and do Thy will, for Jesus' sake. Amen.

LESSON 41

CONFESSION

245. What is Confession?

Confession consists of two parts: the one is that we confess our sins; the other, that we receive absolution or forgiveness from the pastor as from God Himself, in no wise doubting, but firmly believing, that our sins are thereby forgiven before God in heaven.

> I acknowledged my sin unto Thee, and mine iniquity have I not hid. I said, I will confess my transgressions unto the Lord; and Thou forgavest the iniquity of my sin. Ps. 32:5.
>
> If we confess our sins, He is faithful and just to forgive us our sins, and to cleanse us from all unrighteousness. I John 1:9.

246. What sins should we confess?

Before God we should acknowledge ourselves guilty of all manner of sins, even of those of which we are not aware, as we do in the Lord's Prayer. To the pastor we should confess only those sins which we know and feel in our hearts. (See NOTES, *1.* Private Confession, *and 2.* Public Confession.)

247. What are such sins?

Here examine yourself in the light of the Ten Commandments, whether as father or mother, son or daughter, master or serv-

*ant, you have been disobedient, unfaith-
ful, slothful, ill-tempered, unchaste, or
quarrelsome, or whether you have injured anyone by word or deed, stolen,
neglected or wasted aught, or done any
other evil.*

Father, I have sinned against heaven and before thee. Luke 15:8.

This is a faithful saying, and worthy of all
acceptation, that Christ Jesus came into the
world to save sinners; of whom I am chief. I
Tim. 1:15. (Examples of confession.)

NOTES

1. PRIVATE CONFESSION.

In the Roman Catholic Church, Confession is one of
the seven sacraments. Every Catholic must go to Confession at least once a year to remain in good standing as a
church member. His confession is made privately to the
priest. All remembered sins are recounted, and the priest
assigns certain works of penance.

When the Lutherans reformed the practices of the
Church, they retained private confession; not, however, as
a sacrament, but as a privilege. Any Lutheran Christian
whose conscience is burdened with a sin may go to his
pastor and confess his sin privately, and receive absolution.

2. PUBLIC CONFESSION.

In every church service we have public confession and
absolution. See American Lutheran Hymnal, p. 8. The
first two paragraphs are confession, and the third is the
announcement of absolution or forgiveness by the minister.

There is also a service of public confession before every
celebration of the Lord's Supper. Those who intend to
go to communion confess their sins, and the minister an-

nounces to them the forgiveness of sins in the name of the Triune God. This is the form of confession:

O God, our Heavenly Father, I confess unto Thee that I have grievously sinned against Thee in many ways; not only by outward transgression, but also by secret thoughts and desires, which I cannot fully understand, but which are all known unto Thee. I do earnestly repent, and am heartily sorry for these my offences, and I beseech Thee of Thy great goodness to have mercy upon me, and for the sake of Thy dear Son, Jesus Christ, our Lord, to forgive my sins, and graciously to help my infirmities. Amen.

When communion is administered privately to a sick person in his home, a similar form of confession and absolution precedes it.

SCRIPTURE READING

Psalm 51   •

FOR CLASS DISCUSSION

Read Luke 18:9-14. What was the difference between the two men as regards confession? Which one had his sins forgiven? Cannot God forgive sins without our confessing them? Does He? See Explanation of the Third Article. Can He forgive sins if we do not want them forgiven? If we want them forgiven, what will we be willing to do? If we were to confess our sins to God, and forget some of them, would the forgotten sins be forgiven?

PRAYER

This is a faithful saying, that Christ Jesus came into the world to save sinners, of whom I am chief. God be merciful to me, a sinner. Amen.

THE OFFICE OF THE KEYS

248. What is the Office of the Keys?

It is the peculiar church power which Christ has given to His Church on earth to forgive the sins of penitent sinners, and to retain the sins of the impenitent so long as they do not repent. (See NOTES, 1. Office of the Keys.)

> I will give unto thee the keys of the kingdom of heaven; and whatsoever thou shalt bind on earth shall be bound in heaven, and whatsoever thou shalt loose on earth shall be loosed in heaven. Matthew 16:19.

249. What are the words of our Lord Jesus Christ concerning the Office of the Keys?

Thus writes the holy evangelist John in the twentieth chapter: The Lord Jesus breathed on His disciples and saith unto them, Receive ye the Holy Ghost: whose soever sins ye remit, they are remitted unto them; and whose soever sins ye retain, they are retained.

250. What do you believe in accordance with these words?

I believe that when the called ministers of Christ by His divine command deal with us, particularly when they exclude the manifest and impenitent sinners from the Christian congregation, and again absolve those who repent of their sins and are willing to amend—that this is as valid and certain, also in heaven, as if Christ our dear Lord had dealt with us Himself. (See NOTES, 2. Church Discipline.)

> Let a man so account of us, as of the ministers of Christ, and stewards of the mysteries of God. I Cor. 4:1.
> Obey them that have the rule over you, and submit yourselves; for they watch for your souls, as they that must give account. Heb. 13:17. (Passages that show the responsibility of pastors for the souls in their care.)

251. Through whom does the Church administer the Office of the Keys?

Ordinarily the Church administers the Office through its called ministers.

252. How only may the Church use this power?

Only in accordance with the will of the Lord who gave it, that is, to exclude open and impenitent sinners from the Christian congregation, and to forgive those who repent.

NOTES

1. OFFICE OF THE KEYS.

It has this name from the words of Jesus to Peter, "I will give unto thee the keys of the kingdom of heaven" Matthew 16:19. The Roman Catholic Church claims that

St. Peter was the first bishop at Rome (pope), and that the later popes inherited from Peter authority over the whole Church on earth. It is not even certain that Peter was bishop in Rome; but if he was, he was not a pope. There was no papacy until several centuries later. And that the Lord did not give to Peter a power which the other disciples did not have is clear from the passage John 20:19-23, where it is written that He gave the same power to all His disciples. And in Matthew 18:18-20 Jesus says that the power to bind or loose exists wherever two or three are gathered together in His name, for there He is in the midst of them.

2. CHURCH DISCIPLINE.

The power to exclude manifest and impenitent sinners from the Christian congregation is given to the Church. Such exclusion is called the Ban, and the process by which it is arrived at is called Church Discipline. It is described in Matthew 18:15-18. The motive is Christian love, and the aim of discipline is to "gain thy brother." But if he remains impenitent and will not be gained, he is finally excluded. In our Lutheran Church, which has a congregational form of government, the exclusion must be by vote of the congregation. The minister cannot exclude a member by himself.

SCRIPTURE READING

John 20:19-23

FOR CLASS DISCUSSION

When the minister in the church service says, "Almighty God, our heavenly Father, hath had mercy upon us, and hath given His only Son to die for us, and for His sake forgiveth us all our sins"— does everyone who is present receive the forgiveness of his sins? Read the rest of the Absolution and tell who receives forgiveness. When the minister preaches the Gospel, does everyone who hears it receive the forgiveness of sins? Who only is forgiven?

How should Church Discipline be used? (Read Galatians 6:1.) Are we not all sinners? Should we not all be taken into Church Discipline?

PRAYER

I thank Thee, heavenly Father, for the forgiveness of sins in Jesus Christ; and pray that by the power of the Holy Spirit I may ever remain penitent, and therefore forgiven for Jesus' sake. Amen.

PART V

THE SACRAMENT OF THE ALTAR
(or THE LORD'S SUPPER)

The Lord's Supper

LESSON 43

WHAT THE SACRAMENT
OF THE ALTAR IS

253. What is the Sacrament of the Altar?

It is the true body and blood of our Lord Jesus Christ, under the bread and wine, given unto us Christians to eat and to drink, as it was instituted by Christ Himself. (See NOTES, 1. The Lord's Supper.)

254. What do we receive in this Sacrament?

Bread and wine; and in, with and under the bread and wine we receive the body and blood of our Lord Jesus Christ. (See NOTES, 2. Bread and Wine Only, and 3. Body and Blood Only.)

> The cup of blessing which we bless, is it not the communion of the blood of Christ? The bread which we break, is it not the communion of the body of Christ? I Cor. 10:16.

255. Where is it so written?

The holy evangelists Matthew, Mark and Luke, together with St. Paul, write thus:
Our Lord Jesus Christ, in the night in which He was betrayed, took bread; and when He had given thanks, He brake it and gave it to His disciples, saying, Take,

*eat; this is My body which is given for
you; this do in remembrance of Me.*
*After the same manner also He took the cup,
when He had supped, and when He had
given thanks, He gave it to them, saying,
Drink ye all of it; this cup is the New
Testament in My blood, which is shed
for you, and for many, for the remission
of sins. This do, as oft as ye drink it,
in remembrance of Me.* Matthew 26:26-
29; Mark 14:22-25; Luke 22:19, 20; I
Cor. 11:23-26.

256.   When do we have the Sacrament of the Altar?

When bread and wine are consecrated and
distributed to Christians to eat and drink,
according to the institution of Christ.
(See NOTES, 4. The Roman Mass.)

NOTES

1.   THE LORD'S SUPPER.

The Sacrament is called the Lord's Supper because our
Lord instituted it at the evening meal before His betrayal
and death. It is called the Sacrament of the Altar because
it is usually celebrated at the altar. It is called Communion
because by it Christians are brought into union with Christ
and with each other.

2.   BREAD AND WINE ONLY.

The doctrine of some Reformed denominations (non-
Lutheran Protestants) is that the Lord's Supper is only a
memorial feast. They eat bread and drink wine and re-

member Christ's death. It is not, to them, a sacrament which gives the treasures of the Gospel. According to their belief they receive only bread and wine. Therefore a Lutheran should not commune with such a group. (See NOTE 1, Lesson 37.)

3.   BODY AND BLOOD ONLY.

Roman Catholics believe that by the consecration the bread and wine are changed into the body and blood of Christ (transsubstantiation, or change of substance). But St. Paul calls the bread of the sacrament bread, even after the consecration. "The bread which we break, is it not the communion of the body of Christ?" (I Corinthians 10:16). With that one sentence the apostle condemns the false doctrine of both Romanist and Reformed. "The bread which we break"— it is still bread and has not been changed into a different substance; "is the communion of the body of Christ"— those who receive the bread have a communion (sharing) of the body of Christ.

4.   THE ROMAN MASS.

The mass in the Roman Catholic Church is a perversion of the Lord's Supper. The consecrated elements which, according to their belief, are now body and blood of Christ, are not distributed to the congregation, but are offered to God by the priest for the sins of the people. This is called a "bloodless repetition of Christ's sacrifice."

But the letter to the Hebrews says: "We are sanctified through the offering of the body of Jesus Christ *once for all* . . . . for *by one offering He hath perfected for ever* them that are sanctified" (Hebrews 10:10 and 14).

SCRIPTURE READING

Matthew 26:17-30

FOR CLASS DISCUSSION

Jesus says, "This cup is the New Testament in my blood." What is a testament? Look up the words testament, testator, attest, testify. When a court clerk has an important document, like a deed or a marriage license, he affixes the seal of the State to the paper. Why? The New Testament is an important document. The heart of it is the Gospel, the good news that Christ died for our sins. To this document Jesus affixes the seal of the Lord's Supper. Would a court paper be valid without the State seal? Would you ask the clerk to leave off the seal? Why not? Would not the Lord's offer of forgiveness in the Gospel hold good without the Sacrament of His body and blood? But would you want to do without that seal?

PRAYER

I thank Thee, Lord Jesus, that Thou hast given us the Sacrament of Thy body and blood, that, partaking of it in faith, we may be assured that we are one with Thee, dead with Thee to sin, and risen with Thee to life. Amen.

LESSON 44

THE BENEFIT OF THE SACRAMENT

257. What is the benefit of such eating and drinking?

It is pointed out in these words: "Given and shed for you for the remission of sins." Through these words the remission of sins, life and salvation are given unto us in the Sacrament; for where there is remission of sins, there is also life and salvation.

258. To what does Christ refer in the words, "Given and shed for you"?

To His death on the cross for the sins of the world.

> I am the living bread which came down from heaven; if any man eat of this bread he shall live for ever, and the bread that I will give is my flesh, which I will give for the life of the world. John 6:51.

259. What does that mean that we become one with Christ in the Sacrament?

It means that being in Christ who died for our sins, we are without condemnation. (See NOTES, 1. Forgiveness of Sins in the Sacrament.)

> There is therefore now no condemnation to them which are in Christ Jesus. Rom. 8:1.
> Who shall lay anything to the charge of God's elect? It is God that justifieth. Who is he that condemneth? It is Christ that died. Rom. 8:33, 34.

(197)

260.   With what words does the Lord indicate that we
        should frequently commune?

> With the words, "This do ye, as oft as ye
>   drink it."

>> This do ye, as oft as ye drink it, in remem-
>> brance of me. For as often as ye eat this bread
>> and drink this cup, ye do show the Lord's
>> death till He come. I Cor. 11:25, 26.

261.   Why do devout Christians go often to Communion?

> Because they desire the comforting assurance
>   that their sins are forgiven.

NOTES

1. FORGIVENESS OF SINS IN THE SACRAMENT.

In the Apostles' Creed we say, "I believe the forgiveness of sins," and the explanation of that point reads: "In
which Christian Church He daily forgives abundantly all
my sins, and the sins of all believers."

We also learned, under Baptism, that Baptism "works
forgiveness of sins, delivers from death and the devil, and
gives everlasting salvation to all who believe it."

Then, under the Office of the Keys, we learned that
when the minister of God pronounces absolution (forgiveness) to penitent sinners, this is valid also in heaven.

On the day of Communion, therefore, as a baptized
Christian I already have forgiveness of sins. As a member
of the Church I receive daily and abundantly the forgiveness of my sins. In the service of public confession preceding Communion I receive forgiveness. In the liturgy of
the preaching service absolution takes place. And in the
preaching of the Gospel there is also announcement of
forgiveness to all who believe it.

Then comes the Lord's Supper. This Sacrament adds a visible sign and seal. Baptism takes place only once, and perhaps I was too young to remember it. The forgiveness in the Gospel and in absolution are mine, if I believe; but knowing what a sinner I am, my faith is apt to be weak. I believe that God forgives sins in general, but does that mean me in particular? To strengthen our weak faith and assure us of our personal forgiveness, the Lord has added the Sacrament of the Altar. In it He comes to us individually and says, "Yes, my son, my daughter, it means you. As surely as you know that you have received bread and wine, which you have seen, touched and tasted, so surely you may also know that you have received my body and blood which was given and shed for the remission of your sins."

SCRIPTURE READING
Hebrews 10:1-31

FOR CLASS DISCUSSION

Does your father love you? How can you be sure? You know that fathers usually love their children, especially Christian fathers. You know that your father works to supply you with what you need. Does that general knowledge satisfy you? What do you want besides that?

Does a Christian have the forgiveness of sins before he goes to the Lord's Supper? Does he want to go to communion nevertheless? Why?

PRAYER

Lord Jesus, I am Thine and Thou art mine. Renew in me this comforting assurance by the Sacrament of Holy Communion, as often as I partake of it, for Thy love's sake. Amen.

LESSON 45

HOW THE SACRAMENT CONFERS ITS BENEFITS

262. How can the bodily eating and drinking produce such great benefits?

> *The eating and drinking, indeed, do not produce them, but the words, "Given and shed for you for the remission of sins." For besides the bodily eating and drinking, these words are the chief thing in the Sacrament; and he who believes them has what they say and declare, namely, the remission of sins.*

263. What gives the Sacrament its power?

The Word of the Lord Jesus, who instituted it to be used by the Church "till He come."

264. What are the words of the Lord Jesus concerning this Sacrament?

> *"Take, eat; this is My body, which is given for you. . . . Drink ye all of it; this cup is the New Testament in My blood, which is shed for you, and for many, for the remission of sins."* (See NOTES, 1. Consecration of the Bread and Wine.)

265. Why are the eating and drinking important?

   Because the Lord Jesus has connected His
      promise with the eating and drinking,
      and without them there is no Sacrament
      of Communion. (See NOTES, 2. Lutheran
      Doctrine of the Lord's Supper.)

266. Who receives the benefit of the Sacrament?

   He who believes the words of Jesus, "Given
      and shed for you for the remisison of
      sins." (See NOTES, 3. Understanding and
      Believing.)

NOTES

1. CONSECRATION OF THE BREAD AND WINE.

   We do not believe in transsubstantiation, that is, that
the words of the priest change the bread and wine into
body and blood. This doctrine leads to further abuses, as
the worship of the host (consecrated wafer), which they
believe to be the body of Christ; carrying it about in pro-
cession on the festival of Corpus Christi; and withholding
the cup from lay communicants, because "the blood is also
in the body."

   With us the words of consecration are not a magic
charm, but simply a setting apart of the earthly elements
for a holy use in the Sacrament. In this consecration the
minister repeats the words of institution as recorded by the
evangelists, and the Lord's Prayer.

2. LUTHERAN DOCTRINE OF THE LORD'S SUPPER.

   We believe that when we receive the bread and wine
of the Lord's Supper, the Lord also gives us His body and
blood, according to His Word. This is the Lutheran doctrine of the real presence.

3. UNDERSTANDING AND BELIEVING.

We do not understand how the Lord can give us His body and blood. We simply take Him at His Word, and believe it. There are many things we do not understand. We do not know what electricity is, but that does not hinder us from profiting by its many uses. We do not understand how a seed can grow, but we believe it will. When He who is the way, the truth and the life says, "This is my body; this is my blood," we believe Him, and that is all that is necessary.

SCRIPTURE READING

I John 5:1-13

FOR CLASS DISCUSSION

Do the words of consecration which the minister speaks make it a sacrament? What makes it a sacrament? Are eating and drinking necessary? What is a miracle? What is a mystery? Is the Sacrament of the Lord's Supper a miracle? Is it a mystery? Can we decide what the Lord can do or cannot do? Who knows best what He can and will do? What is our part in the Sacrament?

PRAYER

Lord, I cannot understand the working of Thy mighty power, but I can trust Thy love. Whenever I partake of the Sacrament of Thy body and blood, let me do it with the faith of a little child. Amen.

LESSON 46

HOW TO PREPARE FOR THE LORD'S SUPPER

267. Who, then, receives the Sacrament worthily?

Fasting and bodily preparation are indeed a good outward discipline, but he is truly worthy and well prepared who believes these words: "Given and shed for you for the remission of sins." But he who does not believe these words, or who doubts them, is unworthy and unprepared; for the words "For you" require truly believing hearts.

268. What is the outward preparation for the Sacraments?

Fasting and bodily preparation. (See NOTES, 1. Outward Preparation.)

269. What is the true inward preparation?

To desire the forgiveness of one's sins, and to believe that in the Sacrament one receives it through communion with Christ, who died for our sins. (See NOTES, 2. Questions Asked in Confession.)

> Let a man examine himself, and so let him eat of that bread and drink of that cup. For he that eateth and drinketh unworthily eateth and drinketh damnation to himself, not discerning the Lord's body. I Cor. 11:28, 29.

270. Are those of weak faith excluded from the Sacrament?

> By no means; the very purpose of adding a sign and seal to the promise of forgiveness is to strengthen weak faith.

>> Him that cometh unto me I will in no wise cast out. John 6:37.
>> Lord, I believe; help Thou mine unbelief. Mark 9:24.

271. What is meant by "close communion"?

> Because communion is also a public confession of faith, and because there are different doctrines of the Lord's Supper, we believe that Communion should be celebrated only in the company of those who believe as we do. (See NOTES, 3. Announcements for Communion.)

NOTES

1. OUTWARD PREPARATION.

If invited to dine with our friends, we would honor them by presenting ourselves in proper appearance. At the Lord's table we should do no less. Cleanliness, neatness and modesty of dress, and seemliness of behavior should be taken for granted. In addition to this, our fathers often fasted on Communion days, taking no ordinary food before receiving the Sacrament. Luther calls this a fine outward discipline, that is, good training for the body, though it is entirely a matter of choice, and is not required. Our Lord Himself instituted the Sacrament at the end of a meal, and in the early Church it was usually so celebrated.

2. QUESTIONS ASKED IN CONFESSION.

Three questions are asked in the public service of confession in preparation for Communion. He who can honestly answer these questions in the affirmative, and who believes the words of the Lord, "This is my body and blood, given and shed for you for the remission of sins," is worthy and well prepared. The questions are:

Do you truly acknowledge, confess, and lament that you are by nature sinful, and that by omitting to do good and by doing evil you have in thought, word, and deed, grieved and offended your God and Savior, and thereby justly deserved His condemnation? If this be the sincere confession of your hearts, declare it by saying: Yes.

Do you truly believe that Jesus Christ came into the world to save sinners, and that all who believe on His Name receive the forgiveness of sins? Do you, therefore, earnestly desire to be delivered from all your sins, and are you confident that it is the gracious will of your Heavenly Father, for Christ's sake, to forgive your sins and to cleanse you from all unrighteousness? If so, confess it by saying: Yes.

Is it your earnest purpose, henceforth, to be obedient to the Holy Spirit, so as to hate and forsake all manner of sin, to live as in God's presence, and to strive daily after holiness of heart and life? If so, answer: Yes.

3. ANNOUNCEMENT FOR COMMUNION.

In most of our Lutheran congregations, those who wish to go to the Lord's Supper announce their intention to the pastor beforehand. This gives the pastor the opportunity to speak privately with the communicant about his soul's condition — "for they watch for your souls as they that must give account." Heb. 13:17. It also gives the communicant the opportunity to speak to his pastor about anything that is burdening his heart.

SCRIPTURE READING

I Corinthians 11:20-34

FOR CLASS DISCUSSION

Should a Lutheran go to Communion in a Roman Catholic Church? In a church that does not believe in the real presence? Why not? Can little children commune? Give a reason for your answer. Does the fact that the pastor administers Communion to a sick person mean that that person is about to die? If a believer falls ill and dies without having received the Sacrament, is he lost?

PRAYER

Thy table I approach,
   Dear Savior, hear my prayer;
O let no unrepented sin
   Prove hurtful to me there.   Amen.

APPENDIX

THE BIBLE

The salutary doctrine which the Bible contains is briefly comprehended in the catechism.

The title-page of our English Bible reads: "The Holy Bible, containing the Old and New Testaments, translated out of the original tongues, and with the former translations diligently compared and revised, by His Majesty's special command." (This is known as the Authorized Version of 1611.) A revision was later made by English and American scholars. (This is known as the Revised Version of 1881.) Bible means book. Now, since the Holy Scripture is the most important of all books, it is simply called. *"The* Bible," or, *"The* Book."

The Bible is divided into *two parts,* the Old and the New Testaments, or the Holy Scriptures of the Old and New Covenants. Testament or Covenant means the relation of God towards man established by Himself. The Old Testament or Covenant is the relation of God toward Israel established by the giving of the Law at Mt. Sinai. New Testament or Covenant is the designation for the new relation of God towards man brought about by Jesus Christ. Then Testament means the books of the Bible belonging to one or the other of these periods. The Old Testament contains those sacred books which were written by *Moses* and the *Prophets* in the time of the *Old* Covenant, made on Mt. *Sinai.* The New Testament contains those sacred books which were written by the *Apostles* in the time of the *New* Covenant, made on Mt. *Calvary.*

The books of the Old Testament are sometimes divided into Historical books (because *history* prevails in them), Doctrinal [Poetical] books (because *doctrine* [poetry] prevails) and Prophetical books (because *prophecy* prevails).

1. The Historical books are: The five books of Moses (Genesis, Exodus, Leviticus, Numbers, Deuteronomy) Joshua, Judges, Ruth, I and II Samuel, I and II Kings, I and II Chronicles, Ezra, Nehemiah, and Esther.

The *five books of Moses* tell us the story of *mankind* up to the dispersion of nations; the story of the *patriarchs* up to the time of Joseph's death; the story of the *people of Israel* from the deliverance out of Egypt and the giving of the law on Mt. Sinai up to the death of Moses.

> *Note* especially: Gen. 1:1; 3:15; 12:3; 15;6; 32:10, 26; Ex. 19 and 20; 34:6, 7; Lev. 19:2; Num. 6:24-26; Deut. 6:4, 5; 18:18.

The *remaining Historical books* tell us the story of the people of Israel from their entrance into the land of Canaan to the return from the Babylonian Captivity and the rebuilding of the walls of the city of Jerusalem.

> *Note* especially: Josh. 24:15. I Sam. 16. II Sam. 7. I Kings 17:17, 18. II Kings 25. Ezra 6. Neh. 9.

2. The Doctrinal [Poetical] books are: Job, Psalms, Proverbs, Ecclesiastes, The Song of Solomon. The most important of these is the *Book of Psalms.* This was Israel's prayerbook and hymnal. Christians also esteem it very highly. The whole book is often called "The Psalter of *David,*" because 73 of the 150 Psalms it contains are ascribed to David in the headings, and because the singing of Psalms was introduced by David.

> Among the most familiar Psalms are the *Didactic* Psalms: 1, 14, 19; the *Penitential* Psalms: 32, 51, 130; Psalms of *Praise* and *Thanksgiving*: 23, 103, 146; Psalms of the *Cross* and *Consolation*: 42, 91, 126; *Prophetical* Psalms: 2, 72, 110.

3. The Prophetical books are divided into two parts: the Greater and the Minor Prophets. The Greater Prophets are: Isaiah, Jeremiah with Lamentations, Ezekiel and Daniel, in all five books. The twelve Minor Prophets are: Hosea, Joel, Amos, Obadiah, Jonah, Micah, Nahum, Habakkuk, Zephaniah, Haggai, Zechariah, Malachi.

The office of the Prophets was twofold. They were Israel's preachers of repentance and righteousness, who remonstrated with the people because of their defection from God and His law. They also pointed to the coming Messiah and Redeemer. *Isaiah* in particular did this. He spoke as clearly of the future salvation, as though he were standing at the manger and under the cross. He is also called: The *Evangelist* of the Old Testament.

> *Note* especially: Isaiah Chaps. 6, 9, 11, 40, 53, 60. Isaiah (Chaps. 7 and 9) and Micah (Chap. 5) prophesy concerning the *birth* of Jesus. Isaiah (Chaps. 42 and 61) concerning His *office of prophet.* Zechariah (Chap. 9) of His *entrance* into Jerusalem and (Chap. 11) of the *betrayal.* Isaiah (Chap. 53) of Christ's great *suffering* and His everlasting life and kingdom.
>
> *Note.* In some Bibles the *Apocrypha* are inserted between the Old and the New Testament, but they do not belong to the Bible proper. They are called Apocrypha, i. e., hidden books, because the Jews already forbade reading from them in public worship. They are good and wholesome reading, but should not be considered as source and norm of the saving truth.

The sacred books of the New Testament are also divided into Historical, Doctrinal, and Prophetical books.

1. The four Gospels were written by Matthew, Mark, Luke and John. They tell us the sacred story of Jesus Christ; namely, His birth, His life (especially His teaching and miracles), His sufferings and death, His resurrection and ascension. The first three Gospels greatly resemble one another. Luther called the fourth Gospel, "The true, tenderest, chief Gospel." In the clearest manner it testifies that Jesus Christ is God's only-begotten Son.

Note especially: *Matthew* Chap. 2 (the wise men from the east), Chaps. 5-7 (the sermon on the mount), Chap. 13 (parables of the kingdom), Chap. 16 (Christ's church imperishable), Chaps. 24 and 25 (prophecies concerning the destruction of Jerusalem, the second coming of Christ and the last judgment); *Luke* Chaps. 1 and 2 (story of the birth of John and Jesus), Chap. 15 (parables of the lost sheep, the lost piece of silver and the prodigal son), Chap 18 (the Pharisee and publican), Chap. 19 (the story of Zacchaeus), Chap. 23 (of the penitent thief); *John* Chap. 1 (the introduction concerning the eternal Word, that is, the Son of God), Chap. 11 (the raising of Lazarus), Chaps. 14-16 (Jesus' last discourses), Chap. 17 (the sacerdotal prayer).

The *Acts of the Apostles,* written by Luke, tell the story of the *Church* of Jesus Christ; first, its establishment among the *Jews,* especially by Peter (Chaps. 1-12); and then, its establishment among the *Gentiles,* through the missionary journeys of Paul (Chaps. 13-28).

2. *The Doctrinal books* of the New Testament consist of *Epistles* or *Letters* written by Apostles, or men with apostolic authority, to Christian congregations or to individual Christians.

The *Apostle Paul* wrote the first thirteen. They are addressed to the congregations at *Rome* (Italy), at *Corinth* (Greece), in the province of *Galatia* (Asia Minor), in the vicinity of *Ephesus* (Asia Minor), at *Philippi* (Macedonia), at *Colossae* (Asia Minor), at *Thessalonica* (Macedonia), to his co-laborers and disciples *Timothy* (two) and *Titus,* as well as to an individual member of a congregation by the name of *Philemon.* The most important of the Epistles of Paul is his Epistle to the *Romans.* Paul here imparts noble instruction concerning Christian faith and life and proves that we are justified and saved *by grace alone, for Christ's sake, through faith.*

Note especially: Rom. 3:21-28 (of justification by grace alone, through faith in Christ); Rom. 8:1-39 (of adoption,

of consolation amid the sufferings of this present time, of
the certainty of our salvation); I Cor. 13 (of the excel-
lency of love); I Cor. 15 (of the resurrection); II Cor.
5:14-21 (of the atonement); Eph. 6:10-17 (of the Christian's armor).

One letter is addressed to the *Hebrews* (Jewish Christians), but we are not certain as to its author. Of other
Apostles or apostolic men we have one epistle by *James,*
two by *Peter,* three by *John,* and one by *Jude,* the last of
the doctrinal books.

Note especially: Heb. 11:1-12. Jas. 1:12, 22; 2:14-17.
I Peter 2:21-25. I John 2:1, 2, 15-17; 3:1; 4:8, 9, 19; 5:4.

3. The Revelation of St. John is the *Prophetical book*
of the New Testament. It portrays the *struggles* which the
Church of Jesus Christ will have to undergo until the end
of the world, but also the great *victory* to which Christ will
lead His Church. He will lead her to the new heaven and
to the new earth, where she may be with Him alway.
(Chaps. 21 and 22).

THE CHURCH YEAR

The church year is divided into two parts, the festival half and the non-festival half.

In the festival half occur the three great festivals of the Church, Christmas, Easter and Pentecost, and many minor festivals.

Christmas is a fixed festival, coming always on December 25. Easter is a movable festival, and since Pentecost always comes on the seventh Sunday after Easter, it moves with Easter.

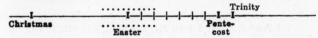

Christ's death and resurrection took place at the season of the Jewish Passover, a feast which was regulated by the moon. Ever since that time Easter has been celebrated on the Sunday after the full moon after March 21. Easter can come as early as the 22nd of March or as late as the 25th of April. The dotted lines in the diagram above represent the space in which Easter may move forward or back. If it comes early, the period between Christmas and Easter is shorter; if it comes later, the period between Christmas and Easter is longer, and the period from Trinity Sunday to the end of the church year is shorter.

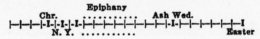

The church year begins with the first Sunday in Advent. There are four Sundays in Advent preceding Christmas; as a result, the first Sunday in Advent is usually the Sunday nearest December 1 (whether in November or December).

Epiphany comes on January 6. The Sundays following are called the Sundays after Epiphany. There may be from three to six Sundays after Epiphany, depending on

(214)

whether Easter comes early or late. The dotted lines in the diagram above represent the Epiphany season.

There are six Sundays in Lent, the period preceding Easter. Lent is a period of forty days, not counting the Sundays. So Lent always begins on the Wednesday preceding the first Sunday in Lent. This is called Ash Wednesday. Before Ash Wednesday there are three preparatory Sundays, called Septuagesima, Sexagesima and Quinquagesima.

Quinquagesima is the Latin word, meaning "fiftieth." It is the fiftieth day, counting back from Easter.

Pentecost is from the Greek word for "fiftieth." It is the fiftieth day, counting forward from Easter.

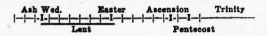

On the fortieth day after Easter comes Ascension Day, celebrating the ascension of Christ to heaven. It is always Thursday.

The Sunday after Pentecost is Trinity Sunday. The Sundays after that belong to the Trinity Season, or the nonfestival half of the church year. They are called simply First Sunday after Trinity, Second Sunday after Trinity, etc. There may be as many as twenty-seven Sundays after Trinity, if Easter comes very early; fewer, if Easter comes later.

The festivals of the church year occur in the following order:

The four Sundays in Advent. Advent means "the coming." The Advent season leads up to Christmas, which celebrates the coming of Christ into our flesh.

CHRISTMAS DAY. The birth of Christ.

Sunday after Christmas (unless Christmas falls on Sunday).

New Year's Day. Commemorates the circumcision of Christ.

Sunday after New Year (unless Christmas falls on Sunday, Monday or Tuesday. New Year's Day falls on the same day of the week as Christmas, just one week later. Since Epiphany is always Jan. 6, if New Year's Day is Tuesday, the following Sunday is Epiphany; and if it is Sunday or Monday, the following Sunday is the First Sunday after Epiphany).

Epiphany. The word means "appearance" or "manifestation," and refers to the showing forth of Christ's glory, especially through the worship of the three wise men.

One to six Sundays after Epiphany.

Three preparation Sundays preceding Lent: Septuagesima, Sexagesima and Quinquagesima.

Ash Wednesday.

Six Sundays in Lent. Lent is a period of forty days of fasting in preparation for Holy Week and Easter.

Holy Week. It begins with the Sixth Sunday in Lent, called Palm Sunday, and includes Maundy Thursday, celebrating the institution of the Lord's Supper, and Good Friday, celebrating the death of Christ for the sins of the world.

EASTER SUNDAY. The resurrection of Christ.

Five Sundays after Easter.

Ascension Day.

Sunday after Ascension.

PENTECOST. The coming of the Holy Ghost. (The day is also called "Whitsunday".)

Trinity Sunday.

Twenty-two to twenty-seven Sundays after Trinity.

Reformation Day. October 31, the beginning of the Reformation.

Thanksgiving Day. The last Thursday in November.

THE HISTORY OF THE CHURCH

1. **The Gospel among the Jews.** Beginning with the day of Pentecost, the birthday of the Christian Church, the Apostles proclaimed the Gospel to their countrymen with great zeal. A great number of the Jews also believed their preaching, so that Jewish-Christian congregations were gathered in Palestine as well as beyond the borders. But the majority of the people hardened their hearts. In A.D. 35, Stephen was stoned, and the Christians were expelled from the temple and the city of Jerusalem. In A.D. 44, James, the son of Zebedee, was beheaded, Peter imprisoned and later Paul was also taken. In A.D. 66, James the Just was killed. Since the Jews rejected their Lord, He also rejected them. *Titus,* the Roman general, advanced against Jerusalem and compassed the city about on all sides. Indescribable distress resulted within the walls by reason of the city being overcrowded with visitors to the Paschal-feast, together with the animosity existing among their leaders. At last Titus conquered the city by assault. *The temple was burned and the walls of Jerusalem made level with the ground.* More than a million Jews had suffered death and about 100,000 were taken captive. *This occurred in A.D. 70.* The blood of Christ had come upon them in a terrible manner.

2. **The Gospel among the Gentiles until A. D. 325.** The proclamation of the Gospel among the *Gentiles* was attended with greater success. When Paul, the great missionary to the Gentiles, was beheaded in Rome (A.D. 67), faith in Jesus Christ was already widely spread in the Roman Empire. Congregations were in existence in Pales-

tine, Syria, Asia Minor, Greece, Italy and Spain. Later on flourishing congregations were organized in Arabia, Egypt, North Africa, Southern France, on the River Rhine and the Danube, and in Brittany. About A.D. 300 there was hardly a district in the Roman Empire which had not been affected by Christianity. In these first times every Christian was actually a missionary, bearing witness of his Savior by word and deed. Nor was the Christian Church allowed to spread so widely without a struggle. There were ten bloody *persecutions of the Christians.* The first occurred in the reign of Nero in Rome (A.D. 64). The Christians, having been sewed in the hides of wild beasts, were thrown before dogs, or, having been coated with wax and pitch, were fastened to high poles in the garden of the Emperor and set on fire in order to illuminate the darkness of night as "living torches." At other times the Christians in France, Egypt, North Africa and Asia Minor were cruelly tortured and persecuted. The last but most atrocious persecution occurred under Emperor Diocletian. But all the power and cunning of heathendom could no longer destroy the Christian Church. The Christians cheerfully laid down their lives for the sake of their faith. Untold numbers died as martyrs, that is, as witnesses to the truth. When the aged Bishop *Polycarp* was asked to curse Christ, he answered: "Eighty and six years have I served Christ, and He never did me wrong; how can I curse my King who will save me!" The most atrocious sufferings were inflicted upon *Blandina.* She was tortured, scourged and lacerated, placed upon a red hot iron chair and at last thrown to wild beasts. In spite of all she confessed and denied not: "I am a Christian; and among us no evil is committed." *Perpetua,* twenty years of age, a lady of rank, was tied to the horns of a wild cow. Though her heathen father on his knees implored and charged her to deny Christ, she remained steadfast, saying: "I am a Christian." New confessors at once took the place of those that were killed, being won to the faith by the courageous faith of the Christians and their cheerfulness in dying. Thus the blood of the martyrs became the seed of the Church. At last Emperor *Constantine* submitted to the divine power of the Gospel. He put an end to the persecutions, permitted men to embrace Christianity and, in the year 325, acknowledged the Christian religion as the religion of the Roman Empire. This was a great advantage because the Christian Church could now develop in quietness and peace. But it also brought with it a great danger because the Church thus lost her freedom and came under the control of the state. The first general Synod, or General Council, the Council of Nice (325 A.D.) was not called together by the Church but by the emperor. The Church had become a State Church.

3. **Internal Conflicts of the Church and further external enlargement.** Hardly had the Church won its victory over the heathen world, before it was deeply agitated by *internal* conflicts. These conflicts were about *pure doctrine*. A man by the name of *Arius* denied the *eternal* Godhead of Jesus Christ, saying that the Son of God also had a *beginning*, that He was a *creature* of God. At the General Council held at Nice in A.D. 325, this false doctrine of Arius was indeed rejected and the Nicene Creed adopted, which reads regarding Jesus Christ: "God of God, Light of Light, Very God of Very God, Begotten, *not made, Being of one substance with the Father*," but the conflict still raged. *Athanasius* was the foremost champion of the true doctrine. Later on *Pelagius* arose and denied the doctrine of original sin. He taught, that man by his *own* power could do good works and merit eternal salvation. This doctrine pronounced the work of Christ and of the Holy Ghost superfluous. Over against this *Augustine* emphasized the Biblical doctrine, that the natural man is totally incapable of good. He taught, and rightly so,

that we are converted and do truly good works alone by the *grace* of God. Notwithstanding these internal conflicts the Church expanded rapidly. The Christian Church won those nations especially, which, coming from the North and Northwest, entered the Roman empire during the Migration of Nations. To *Germany* the Gospel spread by way of Ireland and England.

In the seventh and eighth centuries the Christian Church lost large portions of Asia and North Africa to the Mohammedans, who eradicated the Christian religion and introduced their false religion, called Islam. During this time also the sacred places of Palestine were taken from the Christians.

4. Monks and Monasteries. When a worldly spirit more and more took possession of the Church, many pious men and women sought refuge in solitude from the turmoil of the world. Here, they thought, they could lead a life more pleasing to God. And since they separated themselves from the multitude and lived *solitary* lives, they were called "Monks." When the number of monks grew, they united into communities and built themselves common dwelling places, called *monasteries*. In order that they might lead solitary lives in these buildings, each monk was given a separate cell. The superior of the monastery was called abbot (father). About A.D. 500, Benedict, an Italian, laid down specific rules for the monastic life. Every candidate must undergo a year's probation. Then he must promise to live in *perfect poverty, life-long celibacy and unconditional obedience* to his superiors. Such was the monastic vow. According to monastic rules the monks were obliged to attend common prayer and divine services, to study the Scriptures diligently, to cultivate the land, to instruct the young and to visit the poor and the sick. Thus the monasteries became places of blessing to the Church. But gradually they deteriorated. Enriched by donations, a life of luxury, often even of immorality, was the result. Still the monastic life was regarded as the true Christian life, standing high above the common life and meriting life everlasting. Hence, many noble men and women, who sought rest and peace for their souls and strove after the kingdom of God, entered the monasteries.

5. The Papacy. In the ancient time of the Christian Church the separate congregations were led by Elders (Presbyters). Gradually the presiding officers of the college of presbyters were called "Bishop." Among the bishops again, those of Rome, Constantinople, Antioch, Jerusalem and Alexandria attained to greater prominence. They were called "Patriarchs." Among these again, the bishops of *Rome* succeeded in obtaining the highest position. They claimed that Peter was the Rock upon which Christ meant to build His Church, and that Peter was bishop of Rome. Hence, they called themselves: "Successors to the See of Peter." Rome was at this time the most important city of the known world. The bishops at Rome also wisely decided many questions in controversy submitted to them by other parts of the Church. Relying upon all this, they finally arrogated to themselves the supremacy over the whole Church and demanded that all their decisions be obeyed. As early as the sixth century they received the name of *"Pope"* (father). The Bishop of Constantinople alone refused to submit. Later (A.D. 1054) this led to the *separation of the Greek-Catholic from the Roman-Catholic Church.* Pope *Gregory VII.* (A.D. 1073) especially strengthened the power of the papacy. He forbade the priests to marry, in order completely to separate them from the state and bind them to himself. He forbade the secular princes to invest abbots and bishops and even claimed not to be subject to any ruler, and to have power to remove and appoint emperors. About A.D. 1200 the papacy had attained to its greatest power. This is shown in the *crusades,* which were undertaken by Western princes in the eleventh, twelfth, and thirteenth centuries, in order to wrest Jerusalem and the Holy Sepulchre from the Mohammedans.

Together with the power of the papacy, the *power of error and darkness* increased in the Christian Church. Christ was relegated to the background. His representative on earth, the pope, took the foreground. Among the doctrines it was taught: That man could not stand before God, unless the pope, or the saints, especially Mary, the mother of our Lord, interceded for him; that the priests offered a sacrifice in atonement for the sins of the quick and the dead in the Lord's Supper (sacrifice of the mass); that we are not saved by grace, for Christ's sake, but must *merit* salvation by works; that the priests can prescribe the works by which we can make satisfaction for our sins; that with money we can release ourselves from the punishments of the Church (*indulgences*). They even permitted the people to believe that the forgiveness of sins could also be obtained by money. Through the frequent celebration of the mass the souls of the dead can be saved so much sooner from purgatory, into which all must enter after death for their purification. The *pope* is of *higher authority than Holy Scripture*, for he alone can truly explain this dark book.

6. Martin Luther and the Reformation of the Church. Many a good man had already perceived the corruption of the Church and had fought against it (Peter Waldus in France, John Wiclif in England, John Huss in Bohemia and Savonarola in Italy), but it was by Dr. Martin Luther that the reformation, that is, the renewing of the Church came about.

Martin Luther, the son of a miner, was born on the 10th of November, 1483, in Eisleben in Thueringen, and soon after his birth was taken by his parents from Eisleben to Mansfeld. Here he began his schooling in the Latin school when four or five years old (about 1488-1496), after which he spent a year in Magdeburg and then (1497-1501) continued his studies in Eisenach at the foot of the Wartburg, where he graduated in 1501.

In April, 1501, he entered the University of Erfurt which at that time, with its population of 20,000, was the fifth largest city of Germany, and its University was widely known. Here Luther studied the liberal arts for four years (1501-1505) and received the Master's Degree in January, 1505. Here his daily life was strictly regulated by the University statutes. Regular attendance at the Sunday services was demanded. There was daily reading of a passage from the Bibe and there were prescribed hours for attendance at lectures and for the required preparation. There were also pleasant hours for relaxation, when friends gathered together, and at such times Luther enjoyed playing the lute as a diversion from more serious matters. It was around this time, if not earlier, that he saw a complete Bible for the first time. He was already familiar with the Book of Pericopes, which contained 400 or 500 Bible passages, and had probably bought a copy as early as when he was in Magdeburg, but now he saw a complete copy of the Holy Scriptures. It was in the Library bound to a lectern with an iron chain, so that no one could carry it away but all could read it. It was in Latin, a language that at that time all educated people could understand and speak.

From his earliest years Luther had been religiously disposed and had acquired a goodly stock of Bible verses, Latin hymns, and Bible histories in the Latin School, particularly as a result of singing in the Choir at the daily services. But he had only learned to know Christ as the Judge and not as the Redeemer; as the Judge who would finally return and require of us a strict accounting of all we had done, said, or thought. Even God the Father was not understood by him as the God of Love, who forgives the sinner for Christ's sake, but he knew Him as the stern, uncompromising and punishing God of righteousness who would finally award to every man just what he had earned. This often brought to Luther's mind the question, What must I do that I may stand before such a God? It was a question that particularly troubled Luther about the time that he had passed his examination for the Master's degree and when he, according to his father's wish, was about to begin the study of law.

The crisis came when he was overtaken by a violent thunder storm in a wood at Stotternheim, near Erfurt. The lightning struck near him and, thrown to the ground by the shock, he vowed that if he were spared he would become a *monk*. He shared the common opinion of the day that it was possible to live a holier life in the cloister than out of it and that so it was possible to gain the favor of the divine Judge.

On the 17th of July, 1505, Luther rapped on the door of the *Augustinian Cloister* in Erfurt. It was called the Augustinian Cloister because its regulations were supposed to go back to the Church father Augustine, and Luther chose this particular monastery because it was known for the strictness of its discipline. As soon as his year of probation was completed, Luther solemnly made the three monastic vows and so became an Augustinian monk. Besides participation in the numerous daily services, his duties and privileges included the industrious reading of the Bible, which had been given him when he had made his vows.

Because of his particular talents, his superiors desired Luther to study theology and become a priest. So he familiarized himself with the theology of the Middle Ages, especially with its teaching concerning the mass. On the 4th of April, 1507, he was ordained a priest and celebrated his first mass on the 2nd of May. His father was present on this occasion and so gave his consent to the step his son had taken. Luther's superior, however, was not satisfied to let matters rest here, he wanted him to go further and become a teacher of theology. So Luther had to study the theology of the Middle Ages much more thoroughly than before. During this time he was both a student of theology and also teacher of liberal arts, first in Erfurt (1507-1508), then in Wittenberg (1508-1509), where he had to assist during one school year, at the end of which he returned to Erfurt. In March, 1509, he received the degree of Bachelor of the Holy Scripture, and in the fall of the same year that of a Sententiarius, which carried with it the right to lecture not only on Scriptures but also on the doctrines of the Church. The time from November, 1510, till March, 1511, was spent in a *journey to Rome* which he made in the company of an older Augustinian brother in the interest of business of the order. Here he saw with his own eyes the flippant and godless attitude that prevailed in the "Holy City," the dwelling place of the pope. He never forgot the impressions he received there, but he was still an obedient son of the Roman Church when he returned to Germany.

So Luther had completed six years as an Augustinian monk but he had failed to find what he had sought in the cloister. He had conscientiously observed the monastic rules and often did more than they required. He fasted and chastised his body but did not find peace. The requirement of God that he had not satisfied were continually before his eyes and were always accusing him. When he had fulfilled these requirements in his works and words and conscious thoughts, his tender conscience was still troubled by the fact that the inclination to evil still slumbered in his breast. There were indeed times when he found peace and joy in the cloister, but then the fear of the righteous God, the just Judge, would suddenly overwhelm him, till his soul almost despaired. On one of these occasions an older brother reminded him of the words of the Creed, "I believe in the forgiveness of sins," and his superior Staupitz pointed him to the wounds of Christ that had gained pardon for us. But all that only brought temporary peace. All too soon he again saw God before him with His judging righteousness that told him of nothing except condemnation.

Soon after his return from Rome, Luther was transferred from Erfurt to Wittenberg. Wittenberg had a university since 1502 and some of its teachers were appointed by the authorities of the local Augustinian Monastery. Staupitz assigned Luther as preacher to the Cloister and appointed him to take his place as a professor at the University. As a professor he was to give lectures on the Bible. In October, 1512, he was created a Doctor of Theology with all due ceremony, and in connection with this promotion he had to swear to teach nothing that was condemned by the Church. Among the insignia that were given him was a Bible, first closed and then opened. Later on this became a great consolation to him. When he had to attack the false teachings of medieval theology he was able to say to himself that he was actually maintaining the teaching of the ancient, apostolic Church, and was grounded on the Scriptures to which he was obligated when he was made a doctor. He continued to live in the Cloister, where he also gave his lectures. Beginning in December, 1514, he also preached regularly in the town church as substitute for the invalid pastor.

In 1513 Luther began to hold *Biblical lectures,* which at first were heard only by the monks but soon other students began to attend them. First he expounded the Psalms (1513-1515), then the Epistle to the Romans (1515-1516), then the Epistle to the Galatians (1516), and finally the Epistle to the Hebrews (1517-1518). The first two series of lectures were of special importance because here we find the first evidences of a new understanding of Scripture. What had prevented Luther from finding peace was the fear of God's avenging righteousness. Wherever he read about the righteousness of God in Scripture he thought of it as the righteousness of judgment. For this reason at last he did not like to read the Epistle to the Romans because here there was so much said about the "righteousness of God," (Rom. 1:17). Then, when he was preparing his lecture on the 31st Psalm, he discovered the passage, "Deliver me in Thy righteousness," (Ps. 31:1; 71:2). With these words the Holy Ghost opened his eyes and he said to himself: "If God *delivers* through His righteousness; then there is not only a judging but also a saving righteousness." How can God deliver a sinner and regard him as righteous? This can take place for the sake of Jesus Christ, who has borne the punishment for our sins and fulfilled all of God's requirements. So the one who lays hold on Christ by faith is righteous. Christ's righteousness (that is all that Christ has done and suffered) is imparted to him as his own. With this knowledge Luther was set free from all his anxiety and fear. Now he knew that *the sinner cannot earn for himself the righteousness that he needs to stand before God nor is he required to do so. God Himself has supplied it through Christ, out of pure grace, and it belongs to the sinner as soon as he believes in his heart that Christ is his Savior.* This was an entirely new understanding of the Bible. St. Paul had preached it (Romans 3:21-28) but it had long been forgotten. With apprehension of this understanding the Reformation had its beginning, and from 1513 on, Luther taught it in the circle of his students, in his sermons and in his letters. After the 31st of October, 1517, it was published to the whole world.

In 1506 Pope Julius II proclaimed a jubilee indulgence, which was renewed by Leo X, for the purpose of securing funds for the rebuilding of St. Peter's in Rome. A Dominican monk, Tetzel, one of the vendors of the letters of pardon, came into the vicinity of Wittenberg. We do not know whether he actually used the German rhyme, "Sobald das Geld im Kasten klingt, die Seele (aus dem Fegfeuer) in den Himmel springt." (As soon as the money clinks in the chest, the soul flies up to heaven), but we do know that it was used by some of the peddlers of indulgences and that it was allowed by the Church. Tetzel sold indulgences to the living that guaranteed them absolution from their priest. Many persons in Wittenberg had bought such indulgences. When Luther, as pastor of the city church, insisted, as always, on genuine repentance on the part of those who came to confession, some told him they did not have to repent as they had purchased letters of indulgence. As a result of his indignation over such perversions, *Luther nailed his 95 theses on the door of the castle church in Wittenberg, on the 31st of October, 1517.* In these theses he declared that there is no forgiveness of sins without true repentance, that the forgiveness of sins can never be bought with money, but is freely given to the one who accepts Christ in true faith. Luther nailed these statements on the door of the castle church (which was used as a bulletin board for the University) so that all who could read Latin might be challenged to study the question and to examine the whole practice of selling indulgences. A few weeks later they were followed by a short German treatise on indulgences and grace. The Latin theses and still more the German tract were distributed far and wide as though the angels had carried them about. The posting of the Theses we commonly refer to as *the beginning of the Reformation.*

From that time, one step led to another. First came the personal encounters with Cardinal Cajetan in Augsburg (1518) and with Dr. Eck in Leipzig (1519). Then in many books and tracts, Luther uncovered one false teaching after the other, and showed from Scripture what was the true Christian teaching and the true Christian life. As a result of his proclamation of the truth, Luther was threatened by the pope with excommunication, but he cast the bull into the flames (Dec. 10, 1520) and continued to be unafraid when he was shortly afterwards excommunicated in all due form. He knew that even if he was excluded from the Roman communion he was still a member of the Church of Jesus Christ because this Church on earth includes all those who really believe in Jesus Christ. When at the Diet of Worms (1521) he was asked before the Emperor and princes of the German Empire and the dignitaries of the Roman Church to renounce whatever he had written against the pope and the Roman Church, he boldly answered: "Unless I am convinced by the testimony of Scripture I cannot and will not retract anything. Here I stand, I cannot do otherwise. God help me. Amen."

After the Emperor had declared him an outlaw he was secretly brought to the Wartburg by the Elector of Saxony. *Here Luther began to translate the Holy Scriptures into the German language.* Later Luther fearlessly returned to Wittenberg and there continued his work. He introduced German in place of Latin services, issued a small hymn book, insisted on the establishment of evangelical schools and the thorough religious instruction of the young. In 1529 he wrote his *Small Catechism* for the youth and the common people, his *Large Catechism* for teachers and pastors. A few years before he had issued a collection of German *sermons* that were to show them how and what to preach.

Large numbers of students came to Wittenberg to be prepared by Luther and his co-worker, Melanchthon, for the preaching of the pure Gospel. When they returned to their homes it was to transform their congregations and to give them the knowledge that Jesus Christ was the only

Savior and His grace their only strength. The Church visitations, both in Saxony and in the lands beyond, established well ordered evangelical schools and churches wherever such measures could be carried out. When Luther died (Feb. 18, 1546) the greater part of Germany and Austria had become Evangelical.

7. The Good Confession at Augsburg. The German emperor, Charles V, tried in every way to suppress the preaching of the pure Gospel. When some of the princes and cities protested against his acts at the Diet of Speier (1529) they were given the name of "Protestants." For presentation at the Diet of Augsburg the followers of Luther prepared a short confession of their evangelical faith. It was composed of twenty-eight articles written in their final form by Melanchthon. The main teachings are presented in the first 21 articles, while the abolition of various Roman abuses is defended in the last seven. From the place of its presentation it received the name of the *Augsburg Confession*. It was publicly read before the assembled Diet on June 25, 1530.

The Augsburg Confession and Luther's Small Catechism are the most important confessions of Luther's followers. Where they are confessed and recognized in public teaching and preaching there is the Lutheran Church. Hence June 25, 1530, is sometimes called the birthday of the Lutheran Church, as it marks the rebirth of the pure apostolic teaching in the form of a solemn confession. The Augsburg Confession and Luther's Small Catechism were soon recognized in the greater part of Germany, in parts of Austria and Hungary, and in all parts of Scandinavia.

8. Zwingli and Calvin, the Founders of the Reformed Church. In Switzerland, Ulrich Zwingli preached the Gospel, emboldened by the work Luther did. Unfortunately he did not follow God's Word in all particulars, especially in denying the true presence of the body and blood of Christ in the Lord's Supper. For this reason Luther could not come to an agreement with him at Marburg in 1529. After Zwingli's death (1531) Calvin became in Geneva the central figure of the reformation in Switzerland and France. Though a noble, learned, and God-fearing man he failed to give rightful honor to Holy Scripture in the doctrine of the Word and Sacrament. He also was the chief defender of an erroneous doctrine of election in which he taught that God from all eternity has predestined a part of mankind to salvation and the remaining part to condemnation, in clear contradiction of I Tim. 2:4. Zwingli and Calvin are the fathers of the *Reformed Church*, which spread from Switzerland and France to some parts of Germany, to Holland, England, and Scotland.

9. **The Thirty Years War.** At the Council of Trent, (in Italy) the Roman Church had pronounced its anathemas on the Evangelical Church, thus denouncing both Lutherans and Reformed as heretical. Through the influence of the *Jesuits* the Evangelical Christians were often cruelly persecuted, and in 1618 an actual religious war broke out that lasted for thirty years. In Germany both church and school were almost destroyed and the whole country brought to the verge of ruin. Finally in 1648, chiefly through the intervention of the Swedes (Gustavus Adolphus and his chancellor, Oxiensterna), the *Treaty of Westphalia* was concluded, in which the rights of the Evangelical Church were recognized and confirmed.

10. **The Rebuilding of the Lutheran Church in Germany.** After the end of the Thirty Years War, devoted men in Germany united in their labors to rebuild the devastated Church. Among the most prominent were: Duke Ernest of Gotha, who established Christian public schools in every town and village of his territories; Paul Gerhardt, who gave us so many beautiful hymns and who gave up his fine parish in Berlin rather than give up his

Lutheran faith; Philip Spener, who stressed the fact that true faith is a matter of the heart, that must show itself in a real Christian life; August Hermann Francke (died 1727), who founded the first Orphans' Home at Halle and constantly labored for the education of children in well conducted Christian schools. He was also active in the work of distributing the Bible among the common people and sent the first Lutheran missionaries to heathen lands (India). Later on the Lutheran Church had to go through the period of Rationalism, when human reason (*ratio* means reason) was considered the final authority, in place of Holy Scripture. But, in spite of all that, God's grace preserved the true Church and at the beginning of the nineteenth century raised up His chosen leaders, men like Louis Harms of Hermannsburg, Wilhelm Loehe of Neuendettelsau, and numerous others, who led many back to Luther's faith. So today there is still a Lutheran Church in Germany, Scandinavia, and other European countries. Even the Prussian Union of 1817, that outwardly and forcibly united the members of the Lutheran and Reformed Churches into one Church organization, and confused many consciences, could not destroy it completely. Even today, when many of the organized Lutheran Churches of Europe hardly deserve the name "Lutheran" there are still millions of souls that cling to the faith expressed in the Lutheran Confessions.

11. The Lutheran Church in America. Because Roman Catholic Spain and France first sent their colonists to the newly discovered North America, the Roman Church gained the first foothold. The first Spanish missionaries landed in Florida in 1528 and soon afterwards, in 1534, the French began work along the St. Lawrence in Canada. The Protestant Church arrived a century later. The settlers came chiefly from England and were of the *Reformed* or *Calvinistic* faith. The English came to Virginia in 1607.

Here the Anglican or Episcopal Church became the official Church like the established Church of England. In 1620 the Pilgrim Fathers arrived on the coast of Massachusetts. They were Calvinistic Puritans and accepted the strictly Reformed Westminster Confession in 1648. The Congregationalists, Presbyterians, Baptists, and others are only branches that have grown out of the tree of Calvinism, or the Reformed Church. Even the Methodists, who came into being in England through Wesley (died 1791), and who spread from there to this country, belong to the same stock. In the year 1776 there were in this country about 1950 organized congregations of which 700 were Congregational, 380 Baptist, 320 Presbyterian, 300 Episcopalian, 120 Dutch and German Reformed, 70 Lutheran, 8 Moravian, and 52 Roman Catholic.

The first *Lutherans* came from Holland, from Amsterdam, whence the first shipload of Colonists had arrived in 1623. The *Dutch* founded New Amsterdam (New York) as a Reformed city and colony. There were a number of Lutherans among these emigrants, some from Amsterdam, some from Germany and Scandinavia. The Reformed government, however, did not permit the establishment of Lutheran congregations till 1663. Then the first Lutheran congregations came into existence in New York and Albany. While the language used in the public services long remained Dutch, as the number of German members increased, the use of the German language became general, especially after 1750. The *Swedish* settlements on the Delaware were begun in 1638 and the first Lutheran pastor arrived there in 1640. Though these settlements later passed into the hands of the Dutch and finally, in 1664, came under English rule, they still remained Lutheran. But since the language of the services continued to be Swedish and the majority of the young people only understood English it came about that the congregations were lost to the Episcopal Church. After the conclusion of the Thirty Years War there was an increasing emigration from Europe. This later emigration included not only members of the various sects, (like the Quakers from England and the Mennonites), but also many Lutherans. They settled principally in Pennsylvania, though some went to New York and some to Georgia. The first Lutheran Service conducted in German was held in Germantown, Pa., in 1694, and then a German Lutheran congregation was established in Falckner's Swamp (New Hanover, Pa.). The emigrants from Salzburg, who had been driven from their homeland by the Prince-bishop of the Roman Catholic Church because of their faith, founded the first Lutheran congregations in Georgia in 1734.

Of the greatest importance for the further development of the Lutheran Church in America was the arrival of *Henry Melchior Muhlenberg* in 1742. An appeal for help from the German congregations in Philadelphia, New Hanover, and New Providence had reached the son of August Hermann Francke in Halle. He sent Muhlenberg to them as their pastor. With his arrival a new era began for Lutheranism in America, for Muhlenberg not only administered most excellently the affairs of the congregations that had called him, but he organized new congregations and saw to it that they were provided with competent pastors from Halle, and in addition gathered the newly organized congregations into a Lutheran Synod. As a result, on the 26th of August, 1748, the *Ministerium of Pennsylvania* was organized in St. Michael's Church in Philadelphia. There were only six pastors and a number of lay delegates who then met but it meant that good order was established in the existing congregations, in the instruction of the children, and in the liturgical services. Soon the number of affiliated pastors and congregations increased. The Constitution he had prepared for St. Michael's congregation became the model for later constitutions. Muhlenberg is rightfully called the Patriarch of the Lutheran Church in America.

Later on in other parts of our land Lutheran congregations united in the formation of other Lutheran Synods. So the New York Ministerium was organized in 1786; the North Carolina Synod, 1803; Ohio, 1818; Maryland and Virginia, 1820; Tennessee, 1820. Unfortunately the rationalism of Germany made itself felt about the same time and gained a foothold in many places. Most of the Synods just mentioned united in 1820 to form the General Synod. This body helped to overcome rationalism but did not foster a clear Lutheran confessionalism but rather cultivated fellowship with the surrounding Reformed bodies. This was the reason that in 1867 the Ministerium of Pennsylvania and other synods, under the leadership of Dr. Krauth, separated from the General Synod, and founded the General Council. As the German emigration became smaller in the eastern part of our country, and the children became more and more anglicized, the same change became necessary in the services of the Church so that English more and more supplanted German.

After 1830 the tide of emigration set more to the Middle West and beyond. Here too were many from the Lutheran countries of Europe. The Lutheran Church across the Atlantic did not completely forget the needs of her children, even though it was only in certain circles that this missionary duty was recognized. Most of the work of gathering these emigrants had to be undertaken by the institutions that had been founded in this country for the purpose of supplying them with pastors and teachers. So seminaries were established in Columbus, Ohio, St. Louis, Mo., Dubuque, Iowa, Rock Island, Ill., Chicago, Ill., Minneapolis and St. Paul, Minn. Thence developed our Lutheran Synods: Missouri, Buffalo, Iowa, the Swedish Augus-

tana, and various Norwegian and Danish Synods. Today
the Lutheran Church in our country is chiefly found in three
large groups: The Synodical Conference (Missouri, Wis-
consin, and several smaller Synods), The United Lutheran
Church in America (composed of the former General
Synod, General Council, and United Synod of the South),
and the American Lutheran Conference (including the
American Lutheran Church, Norwegian Lutheran Church,
Augustana Synod, United Danish Lutheran Church, and
the Norwegian Free Church). The bond that unites them
is the confessions of the Church and the Common Service
that is finding ever greater acceptance. What still separates
them is the fact that not all adhere to the Confessions and
to Lutheran practice in the same way. The Church in this
country is still one of mnay languages and will have to
continue to be so for some time but her official language is
that of the land in which she carries on her work, whose
protection she enjoys, and for whose blessing she is called
to labor. One of the greatest blessings our country affords
the Church is the fact that there is not a state church, but
that the Church is free to carry on her activities inde-
pendently and to order her life freely, according to Scripture and the Confessions.

CHURCH MEMBERSHIP AND WORK

"It is the Christian's duty to unite with a faithful congregation, and do his part in all its work."

The congregation's work is of two kinds: that which it does in its own neighborhood, and the world-wide work which it does by cooperating with other congregations.

THE LOCAL WORK

The local congregation must see to it that the Word of God is preached and taught in its own community. To this end it builds a church, calls a minister, and supports him so that he can give his whole time to the work.

It also operates one or more schools (day school, Sunday school, daily vacation Bible school, pastor's confirmation class) where the Bible is taught, especially to children and young people.

Nearly every congregation also has organizations for special groups among its members, such as Luther League (for young people), Women's Mission Society, Men's Brotherhood, and others.

In all of its work the Christian congregation has one aim, to spread the Gospel according to the command of the Lord Jesus: "This Gospel of the kingdom shall be preached in all the world" (Matthew 24:14). By bringing the Gospel to all men the Church hopes to win them for Christ and for heaven.

All of the work of the Church is supported by the free-will offerings of its members. Giving is a part of Christian living.

THE WORK AT LARGE

Preaching the Gospel in all the world is too large an undertaking for any one congregation. To accomplish the larger tasks of the Church, many congregations must work together.

One of the larger duties of the Church is Christian higher education. If we are to have colleges where we can be sure that Christian young people will be taught by Christian instructors, the Church must provide them. To obtain a constant supply of ministers for the congregations, the Church must have seminaries to train young men for the ministry.

Another important work of the Church at large is the publishing of Christian literature. The Church has its own publishing houses which print and distribute Bibles, catechisms, Sunday school literature, Christian papers and magazines.

Foreign mission work is very important if the Gospel is to be preached in all the world. Missionary pastors and teachers, Bible women, doctors and nurses are trained and sent out to foreign countries to bring the good news of salvation to the heathen.

Even in our own land there is home mission work to be done besides that which each congregation does in its own neighborhood. To call pastors to work in communities where there is no congregation, to erect a place of worship and gather a congregation there, is possible only through the cooperation of many self-supporting congregations.

Then there is the charitable work of the Church, caring for the aged, the orphans, the sick in various homes and hospitals. One congregation alone could not accomplish much, but many working together are able to supply all that is needed.

All this larger work of the Church, like that of the home congregation, is kept up through the free-will gifts of Christians. "God loveth a cheerful giver" (II Corinthians 9:7).

CHURCH MEMBERSHIP

Every real Christian wants to take part in the work which the Church is doing — Christ's work. To do this, it is necessary for him to join a local congregation.

It is through the local congregation that the Christian keeps in contact with the means of grace. The believer knows that without that contact his Christian life will dwindle and disappear. Therefore he is careful to maintain a regular attendance at God's house and to commune frequently.

Within the local congregation many opportunities for service are given. The earnest Christian will be glad to make the most of these opportunities, and thus make his life count for God. He may serve as member of the church vestry, teacher or officer in the church school, officer in one of the organizations, delegate to conventions, member of a working committee, sponsor of a Boy Scout troop, member of the church choir, organist, musician in an orchestra, director of recreational activities, and in other ways. Every talent may be consecrated to the Lord. "Whatsoever thy hand findeth to do, do it with thy might."

Above all, and through all other service that he renders, the Christian is a missionary. By his life and his testimony he is persuading other men to "taste and see that the Lord is good," that they also may "know the love of Christ which passeth knowledge."

In all this work, both that of the home congregation and that of the Church at large, the Christian participates in three ways:

1. He gives himself. His time, his talents and his labors are freely given to the Lord of the Church in whatever way he can be of service.

2. He gives of his wealth. All that he has comes from God, and he is glad to give as God has prospered him.

3. He gives his prayers. Even those who cannot give much or go far in the service of the Church can take part in all of its world-wide work through their prayers.

"But grow in grace and in the knowledge of our Lord and Savior, Jesus Christ. To Him be glory both now and forever. Amen." (II Peter 3:18).

Sacriment. ① Command.
② earthly element.
③ heavenly gight of grass

chuch history is a subjec
as hard as I can he.
first it killes the
deciepples and now
it killing me.